kapihan

A Celebration of Coffee in the Philippines

The universality of coffee: from the lobby of the Manila Hotel...

kapihan

A Celebration of Coffee in the Philippines

KAPIHAN
A Celebration of Coffee in the Philippines
Nestlé Philippines Inc. © 2007

Author: Noel Sy-Quia

Photographer: Neal Oshima

Copyeditor: Arnold Moss

Book and Design Development: Tina Colayco

Designer: Aman Santos

Map Illustration: Ava Salazar

Publication Director: Melody Gocheco
Project Coordinator: Saira Peñaranda
Repro and Print Production: John Phang

Produced and Designed by ArtPostAsia Pte Ltd
Email: publications@artpostasia.com
www.artpostasia.com

Printed in Malaysia
First Edition 2007

ISBN 978-971-93896-1-3

Coffee's range: From staged elegance...
to the back of a jeepney.

Coffee served in traditional coffee trays.
Bangkerohan Public Market, Davao City.

*Start of day, jockeys make sure they stay sharp
in the saddle at the Sta. Ana race track.*

CONTENTS

NESCAFÉ was launched in 1938 by Nestlé. It arrived on Philippine shores in the ration packs of American soldiers during World War II, and soon made its way into households, restaurants and *kapihans* all over the country.

We are proud of our long and deep association with the Philippines. For most citizens, NESCAFÉ has become a constant companion at breakfast, and throughout the rest of the day. We delight in being part of so many personal memories, reaching back in time to parents, grandparents and even great-grandparents. To us, it has been a history of our consumers' consistent loyalty and appreciation. New coffee products, developed over the years to meet the changing needs of our consumers, have readily found a place in their daily lives. New research findings on the numerous health benefits of coffee have been specially rewarding, giving our work and products added relevance. We have noted our consumers' increased awareness of health and wellness, and have responded accordingly. We now make available a wealth of pertinent information to help consumers make their choices, from coffee's qualities as a rich source of antioxidants to evidence linking coffee with disease avoidance.

We are pleased with our relationships with coffee producers in the Philippines. Thirty thousand farmers and another 300,000 individuals are involved in the coffee supply chain, from seed to cup. It is a relationship marked by mutual dedication, benefit and support. Investments by NESCAFÉ in agricultural research, farmer training and technology transfer continue to make important contributions in quality, yields and risk management for the farmer. Our long-established practice of buying directly from farmers has brought openness to the national coffee market.

This dedicated attention to our consumers and support of our suppliers have earned NESCAFÉ its presence in Philippine life.

My regular travels to different parts of the country are gratifying as I witness recognition of our brand by consumers, and our product's fulfillment of their expectations for quality.

This book is dedicated to all who have contributed to the success of NESCAFÉ: the hard-working Filipino farmer, the appreciative consumer and the committed team of NESCAFÉ professionals who bring the two together.

NANDU NANDKISHORE
Chairman and CEO
Nestlé Philippines, Inc.

Personal mugs line the shelves, waiting for regular customers at a market coffee shop, Iloilo City.

coffee, coffee everywhere

*Studying form over coffee at the
Sta. Ana racetrack.*

A Jeepney driver enjoys his regular morning cup of instant coffee as he prepares to take on the EDSA rush hour, taking commuters to their offices, where more coffee awaits in corporate canteens and meeting rooms.

Cups of coffee turn up in any context, at any time. Early in the morning it is poured in the intimacy of one's kitchen, the clatter of the market kapihan or the hush of the café. Jeepney drivers on EDSA rush through their cups of instant coffee before taking commuters to their offices, where more coffee awaits in corporate canteens and meeting rooms. As the day progresses, coffee continues to make its appearance in supporting roles to meals and snacks, or as solo acts. It helps the hum of solitary thought, or prompts the flow of *kwento* and *tsismis*. Home supplies can be replenished anywhere, from a rack in the *sari-sari* store or the shelf in an air-conditioned supermarket. Late at night, it accompanies call-center employees, relaxed diners and students cramming for that morning exam.

Coffee lends itself to many purposes. It is both sword and shield in handling stress. Early in the morning it arms against the strains of the day, late in the afternoon it marks the start of a well-earned break. It is a source of livelihood to over 30,000 growers, and to hundreds of thousands more traders, roasters, café owners and corporate employees. Coffee engages a wide range of energies, from the preoccupations of farmers and agronomists to the creativity of culinary chefs and interior designers. In Benguet Province of Northern Luzon, coffee has woven itself into the community life of the Igorot, where it is accorded its own ritual. To individuals like Chit Juan, co-chairman of the Philippine Coffee Board, and coffee entrepreneur Patrick Joson of Kape ni Juan, coffee has become an anchor of national identity and source of pride.

Whether intimate or sociable, brother-in-arms or comforting nurse, as part of personal or tribal ritual, source of livelihood or pleasure, or even national rallying cry: coffee is everywhere, and everywhere performs its called-upon duty.

Rush hour at the counter: One's work is another's break.

Opposite: Off to a great start. Maybe dinner after two more coffee dates? Salcedo Park, Makati City.

'Green coffee' volumes are measured in 60-kilogram bags.

Opposite: Green coffee beans, coffee powder, and roasted coffee beans.

coffee's long road
to the philippines

Filipino Coffee Company, Pike's Peak Market, Seattle, 1909. Seattle's Starbucks opened its first location in Manila in 1997.

Legend has it that the discovery of coffee was due to animal intervention. A goat in the Ethiopian province of Kaffa — whose capital Jimma lies on the same latitude as Dumaguete in the Philippines — first discovered the joys of eating the red berries of the coffee tree. Curious about the goat's liveliness, the goatherd tried some berries himself. So begins the human history of coffee. Its travels throughout the world and to the Philippines were marked by events ranging from religious devotion to skullduggery. Coffee's first departure from Ethiopia most probably took place, sometime between the 6th and 9th centuries, at the port of Aseb in present-day Eritrea, on the narrowest stretch of the Red Sea. On the far shore lies Mocha, a port in southwestern Yemen, 45 miles away. How it made the initial crossing is the subject of dispute. A Sufi grand master, Ali ben Omar al-Shadili, founded a monastery in Mocha, and valued coffee for its ability to keep worshippers awake at night. Coffee soon spread across Muslim clerical communities, making its way to Mecca by the 15th century. The jump into secular life happened quickly enough, and coffee traveled with Muslim armies into southern Spain, North Africa and India. Turkey developed its own coffee culture after the addition of Mecca to the Ottoman Empire in the 16th century.

A merchant brought coffee to Venice in 1615, creating the European market. The Venetians dominated the coffee trade into Europe for about a century, and this caught the eye of merchants in Amsterdam, often referred to as the Venice of the North. Suppliers on the Arabian Peninsula had not allowed any coffee plants to leave their shores, and all exported beans were either grilled or boiled to keep them from germinating.

Legend inserts itself again. It is told that Baba Budan, an Indian Sufi saint, turned smuggler upon leaving the Peninsula with unprocessed green coffee beans strapped to his body in the 1600s. He is credited with bringing coffee cultivation to India, and beyond. Another wave of dispersion was kicked off by the Dutch. A coffee plant, whether a descendant of Baba Budan's seeds or not, was taken to Amsterdam in 1616. A coffee plantation opened on Dutch-owned Java at the end of the century, and the first bean shipment was made in 1706. The European market expanded further.

The mayor of Amsterdam gifted a coffee tree to Louis XIV in 1714. In 1720 de Clieu, a Martinique-based infantry officer, was visiting Paris. He asked for a cutting of the tree for

Coffee jumped the Red Sea into Yemen at its narrowest point.

planting on the Caribbean island, but the request was denied. Determination prevailed, and he jumped over the garden walls at night to help himself. During a perilous return voyage, the ship's water had to be rationed; he poured his scarce supply on the cutting, to ensure that his coffee plant would survive. It was the start of coffee cultivation in the French colonies.

Coffee consumption continued to grow. Seven years after de Clieu's acts of thievery and sacrifice, it was Brazil's turn to want to enter the coffee market. Seeds were needed, but no one supplied them willingly. Lieutenant Colonel de Melo Palheta was given the mission to secure them. He traveled north to French Guyana pretending to be on a diplomatic mission. Access was impossible into fortress-like coffee farms, even at night. Instead, he seduced the governor's wife. At a state dinner he was presented with a bouquet of flowers. Hidden inside it were coffee seedlings, offered in gratitude for attentions rendered. Coffee was now set to become a mass market. Spanish-administered Latin America soon had its own share of plantations, and it was from Mexico that a Franciscan friar brought the first coffee seeds to the Philippines — in Lipa, Batangas in 1749.

Coffee had to travel over Spain and through Mexico before reaching the Philippines.

Public places with tables, chairs, and food: coffee is always at hand.

WORLD WAR II:
THE START OF LARGE-SCALE COFFEE CONSUMPTION IN THE PHILIPPINES

In 1930 the Brazilian Coffee Institute approached Nestlé with a request. Brazil had been building up surplus stocks of coffee, and beans often had to be destroyed to keep prices from getting punitively low. Could Nestlé develop a product that could make commercial use of surplus stocks? Nestlé started to search for ways to further broaden the demand for coffee worldwide. It needed to make coffee preparation and consumption possible in new contexts, and with greater ease. Eight years of research led to the development of soluble coffee powder. It met the key criteria of access and convenience: a cup of coffee prepared with minimum handling, equipment and time, and with maximum shelf life. Coffee could now be served in more places more easily, from time-constrained homes to polar expedition camps, or even the battlefield mess tents. Nestlé became a supplier to the US military, and World War II accelerated the introduction of this new product, Nescafé. Annual production reached one million cases in 1943. Nescafé reached the Philippines the year after.

It was a few minutes after 10:00 a.m. on October 20th, 1944, when US troops first landed on Leyte. With the beachhead secured, the Battle for Leyte Gulf raged on from the 23rd to the 26th in the air and at sea, and one can imagine troops and commanders relying on "instant" coffee to keep sleep at bay and senses sharp. It was 106 days after the Leyte Landing when American forces entered Manila on the morning of February 3. Nescafé's introduction to the Philippines had begun.

When it first appeared in the Philippines, this can was a novelty. A generation later it was the stuff of nostalgia.

Afternoon coffee business at Agdao Public Market, Davao City.

Opposite: Eight years of research led to the development of instant coffee.

Coffee helps the hum of solitary thought, or prompts the flow of (local gossip) 'kwento' and 'tsismis.'

Opposite: Nescafé's advertisement anchor many childhood and adolescent recollections.

THE BEST POSSIBLE START

The backdrop of World War II was unfortunate, but a business-school student would find it extremely difficult to pick a better moment for introducing Nescafé to the country. Collective euphoria, release from the accumulated stress of occupation and an association with the liberator marked the introduction of Nescafé to its first consumers in the Philippines. Commercial operations soon followed, and the rest, as is often said, is history.

Filipinos whose relatives lived through World War II recall their grandparents' taste for Nescafé. Looking back, one notices how their friends shared the same fondness, and how it carried with it the new-found optimism of the post-war years. Their appreciation became their children's, and in time subsequent generations created their own associations and memories. Nescafé commercials anchor many a childhood and adolescent recollection. To remember fondly the celebrity of a past Nescafé commercial is to mark one's age. Nescafé glass jars found all manner of uses beyond coffee: storage for mechanics' nuts and bolts, jewelers' beads, *sari-sari* candies, storage for that home-made *sawsawan*, even transportation for goldfish. The 50-gram diamond jar was even seen in non-Nescafé commercials, and was part of many a Ginebra-toasting

scene in movies. It is part of the national fabric: one expects to see Nescafé in kitchen cupboards, on supermarket shelves, in restaurants, *kapihans* and *sari-sari* stores, even in the remotest parts of the archipelago. Today, to find it is reassuring; not to find it is surprising.

Green coffee berries ripening on a tree.

where it all starts

Note the lighter shade of the shoots at the end of the branch. These are tender enough to eat.

Opposite: Red berries signal ripeness - these need to be picked, the rest left on the branch to ripen.

THE COFFEE PLANT

LEAVES

Leaves have a waxy surface. They contain caffeine, and in some coffee-growing cultures they are used for making tea. Young shoots are edible raw, and share the astringency and taste of their guava counterparts. Some farmers like to cook the shoots and season them with salt.

FLOWERS

The white flower is made up of a five-toothed outer calyx and a five-part inner corolla. In both appearance and smell it can be reminiscent of the jasmine bloom. Arabica flowers after a rain, while Robusta flowers bloom irregularly. Flowers last a few days. Workers tending coffee trees often eat a bloom — a pleasant mix of nectar and caffeine — to raise their energy levels.

BERRIES

The coffee berry typically grows to a diameter of 15 to 35 millimeters. In relative size, Robusta beans are small, Arabica medium and Liberica large.

The berry turns red as it ripens, with a bright red color signalling ripeness and readiness for picking. It can turn brown to reddish brown afterward and, in the case of Arabica, will fall off the tree.

The outer skin of the coffee berry is generally tough, and covers a slightly sweet, soft inner pulp that is pleasant to chew when ripe.

Each berry contains two seeds. Some berries, known as peaberries, have been known to contain just one large seed. Removal of the outer hull yields the green coffee beans, which require drying prior to roasting and grinding in preparation of coffee. It takes 8,000 beans to make a kilo of roasted coffee.

Wavy edge, waxy surface: coffee trees are easy to spot, even when growing wild. From left to right: Liberica, Excelsa, and Robusta.

LEAVES

Hints of jasmine and citrus. If the berries were not so sought after, coffee blooms would appear in flower arrangements.

FLOWERS

How picky is the picking? Look inside the
picker's basket: if entirely red, then only the
ripest berries have been selected. It'll show
up in the taste of the coffee.

BERRIES

COFFEE VARIETIES

Botanically, the coffee plant belongs to the Rubiaceae family, genus *coffea*. There are over 30 varieties of the genus, but four commercially grown varieties: Arabica, Robusta, Liberica and Excelsa. Of these, Arabica and Robusta are the two dominant varieties in the world market. Arabica commands a 70% share of the world market, with Robusta claiming 30%. Excelsa's and Liberica's shares are negligible. The Philippines distinguishes itself by growing all four varieties. In 2005 and 2006 Robusta accounted for 71%, Arabica 20%, Excelsa 8% and Liberica 1% of national production.

ARABICA

Known as *kapeng tagalog*, coffee brewed from Arabica beans is described as being aromatic, rich and delicate, with a measure of acidity providing a sharp, pleasing and balanced flavor that tends to neither sour nor sweet. The flavors of the Arabica bean tend to become more concentrated when growth is slow, as happens at altitudes over 1,200 meters, making it a favored variety in the Luzon Cordillera.

ROBUSTA

As its name suggests, Robusta is a more disease-resistant variety, especially against the feared coffee rust blight, *hemileia vastatrix*, which devastated the Philippine coffee industry at the end of the 19th and the start of the 20th centuries, and to which Arabica is vulnerable. It is also a high-yielding variety. It contains 50% more caffeine than Arabica, and its taste is referred to as being stronger. To wine tasters, Arabica might be "fruit"; Robusta, the "tannins" that shape the wine and give it "structure." The stronger-flavored Espresso blends typically include Robusta.

Ripe beans remain on the tree, reducing its requirement for maintenance. It grows best at lower elevations below 900 meters.

LIBERICA OR *BARAKO*

Liberica is known as *kapeng barako*. The term *barako* means male animal or stud. It hints at masculine vigor, an attribute associated with the coffee's flavor. This is described as "strong," "earthy," "pungent" and of "powerful body." It produces the biggest berry of the domestically grown coffee varieties, and some hint that it is this feature that earns it the name *barako*. It tolerates drought. Its hull is more difficult to remove, and this characteristic has also earned it the name *kapeng makapal*. Liberica or *barako* is now predominantly grown in Cavite Province, where it does well at lower elevations. Its leading export market is the Middle East.

EXCELSA

Excelsa beans are cultivated in the same areas as Robusta. It has a distinct *langka* (jackfruit) taste. It features prominently in a blend known as Kalinga Brew, in which it is combined with Arabica and Robusta beans. It grows in Basilan and other parts of Mindanao.

Sun-drying: A key step prior to processing.

The sound made when shaking a fistful of dried coffee cherries gives an indication of their moisture content.

Opposite (from top to bottom): roasted beans, husked 'green' Arabica beans, and instant coffee, ready for the cup.

Instant coffee, like any other kind, is produced from roasted and ground beans. The resulting coffee has its water removed – either through the heat of spray-drying, or through freezing – to produce the soluble powder. This last step is what distinguishes instant from traditionally prepared coffee. For instant coffee, only hot water needs to be added to produce a cup. For roast and ground, coffee has to be steeped in hot water for brewing, and its grounds disposed of when used. The convenience and speed of preparing instant coffee make it a very compelling choice: no coffee-brewing jug is needed, and there are no waste grounds to dispose of when done. This becomes particularly evident when preparing iced coffee, as instant coffee powder is equally soluble in cold water or milk.

It is true that coffee essences and aromas may be lost during the spray-drying or freeze-drying process, but these are captured and reintegrated into the soluble powder. Interestingly, instant coffee stays fresh and retains its flavor much longer than its roast and ground counterpart.

When it comes to caffeine content, instant coffee tends to contain approximately 60% to 80% of the caffeine contained in roast and ground coffee, whose caffeine concentration can vary significantly by preparation method. A cup of coffee is usually understood to be a volume of 150 ml. For this volume, instant coffee contains an average of 65 mg of caffeine. Roast and ground coffee prepared by the drip method contains an average 115 mg, percolated coffee an average 80 mg. This relative difference in caffeine content has created two patterns of habit. Regular instant coffee drinkers can, and often do, consume a higher volume of prepared coffee. Those who like to drink roast and ground often opt for a cup of instant at the end of the day, especially when they feel they are close to being 'maxed out' on caffeine, but want to carry on drinking coffee.

Animal-processed beans: these beans have journeyed through the alamid's digestive tract, and can sell well above market prices for premium coffee.

FELINE COFFEE CRAVINGS

Coffee doesn't appear to be the sole enjoyment of Homo sapiens. An Ethiopian goat seems to have discovered it first and brought it to human attention. Another animal consumer — a particularly discerning one — is the civet cat, known generally as *alamid* (Tagalog), and as *motit* (Kankana-ey) in the Mountain Province of Northern Luzon. A solitary night forager, it feeds on the ripest coffee berries in the wild, digesting the fleshy hull and excreting whole coffee beans. These can be found in clusters on the forest floor or in the fields during the day. Talk to anyone who grew up in a coffee farming community, and chances are they will have had some experience of *alamid* coffee. Francisco Laigo, a pest-control expert working for Chiquita Unifrutti in Cagayan de Oro, recalls growing up in the Luzon Cordillera. From the age of seven, he and his brothers took turns in scanning the fields at dawn for the discarded beans. Five to six sticky clusters were enough for a pot of coffee. "That is the best coffee," he says emphatically, his face set in happy recollection. The resulting brew is described as being richer in taste; some

detect added chocolate notes in its aroma, with a cleaner aftertaste and an absence of bitterness. How the link was made between excreted beans and extraordinary coffee is the subject of speculation, and there is little agreement on the likely causes of the resulting taste of *alamid* coffee.

Some point out that the cat selects only the ripest, tastiest cherries, and that commercially produced coffee is a mix of ripe and less-ripe beans. Researchers at the University of Guelph in Ontario, Canada, found that *alamid* coffee was lower in protein — which gives coffee its bitter taste — following its interaction with gastric acid and enzymes in the cat's stomach.

It appears to be a rare instance of cross-species collaboration resulting in a "win-win" outcome: the cat feeds on the hull, man enjoys a better cup of coffee, or gets to sell it at over 10 times the price of coffee processed entirely by humans.

Checking seedling quality and progress.

GROWING COFFEE

Coffee has many attractions for the farmer. It benefits from growing demand: world consumption grew 33% over the last decade. Current prices make cultivation economically attractive. Once productive, the coffee plant requires relatively little care. Being a tree, it holds the soil in place and does not require plowing like other crops, thereby avoiding soil erosion. It is virtually imperishable once harvested and processed into green beans. This makes it a suitable crop for remote areas where produce cannot be rushed to market right after harvesting.

As with all agricultural products, coffee carries its own risks. As the second most traded commodity after oil, coffee is subject to world prices. While demand has grown steadily, supply has grown unevenly, causing serious fluctuations in price. 1994 saw a peak price of 155 US cents per pound and then went down to 19 cents in 2002. One major cause of this dramatic price reduction was the tremendous growth in Vietnamese coffee production. While world consumption grew by a third over the last decade, Vietnamese exports and world market share tripled, propelling it from seventh to second place — behind Brazil — among top producers. The world market now appears to have absorbed Vietnamese production fully. With supply once more tracking demand, prices make coffee growing attractive again.

Assuming prices are attractive, the farmer's concern is about maximizing the quality and quantity of yields. This requires care and attention in selecting and maintaining plants. Adequate land preparation, planting and tree life cycle management approaches, let alone best practices in pruning, fertilization and weed and pest control are needed to ensure optimum outcomes. Harvesting and post-harvest treatment require attentive care too as errors can affect the marketability of beans. Finally, there is the risk of selling itself, of making sure that the best possible price is being applied to the correctly assessed quality of beans. Uninformed sellers risk exploitation in the hands of unscrupulous buyers.

Nescafé, the largest coffee brand in the Philippines, also shares such risks. Negative outcomes in farming directly affect the volume and quality of raw material arriving at its factory gates in Cagayan de Oro. Every farmer, discouraged from continuing to grow coffee because of temporarily depressed prices forces Nescafé to import from abroad. Nescafé buys 80% of Philippine farmers' output of coffee beans. The shared interest in dealing with these common issues is significant, and Nescafé has invested accordingly to address them.

Healty nursery habits: early selection, precision, consicentious and competent care ensure good harvest and good coffee.

The space between coffee trees can be taken up by other crops, like peanuts, that do not compete for nutrients. This kind of intercropping provides additional income to farmers.

Opposite: Canopies provide shade, slowing down water evaporation for the young plants.

The coffee berry typically grows to a diameter of 15 to 35 millimeters.

Opposite: A discerning picker at work, precision and patience ensure quality.

Knowledgeable and careful land preparation shortens the time to first harvest, and maximizes yields.

THE SCIENCE OF COFFEE FARMING

"It's like choosing your spouse-to-be
while wearing a blindfold."

- Zenon Alenton, Nescafé Agronomist,
warning against choosing a coffee
tree whose genetics are unknown.

The Nestlé Experimental and Demo Farm spreads out over 16 hectares in Mindanao. It functions as a research center, training facility and showcase for coffee farming. It also raises ready-to-plant seedlings in its nurseries. Zenon is its resident agronomist. One of the most gratifying aspects of conducting research for this book was the universal enthusiasm that people, whether consumer or professional, showed for coffee. Zenon's zeal ran deep. It became clear very quickly that he knew every tree individually. I did not ask, but suspect he knew them all by name.

Nescafé embarked on its worldwide Sustainable Agriculture Initiative in 2003, and its principles can be seen at work on the farm, which follows the coffee-specific '4Cs' guidelines. The Common Code for the Coffee Community Association promotes sustainable production, processing and trading of green coffee. Its specific aims are to bring about continuous improvement of the social, ecological and economic conditions of coffee producers, while ensuring the quality of their product. It also incorporates the objective of helping farmers to manage the potentially negative impact of fluctuating coffee prices.

Coffee trees have a life span of 50 years, which makes it important to plant the most productive, as well as most disease-and pest-resistant strains. Zenon draws the parallel with choosing one's spouse at every training session he hosts. The farm is part of a continuous, comprehensive research program to identify the coffee trees best suited for production. Seedlings raised from such strains are sold to farmers at cost. Planting from these incurs a waiting time of 18 to 20 months before harvesting the first crop. Traditional planting from seed can impose a five-year wait.

To manage the risk of fluctuating coffee prices, farmers are advised to plant their trees to allow the planting of additional crops, a practice known as intercropping. Typically, coffee trees are planted two meters apart in rows, and three meters across from neighboring rows. This results in a tree density of 1,667 trees per hectare. To allow intercropping, tree rows are planted 5 meters apart, leaving room for a parallel crop. This allows 1,000 trees to be planted per hectare. Particularly suitable

intercrops that do not compete with coffee for nutrients range from *ampalaya* to peanuts and *ube*. Peanuts, for example, can yield up to 5,000 kilos of product per intercropped hectare, providing income while the coffee trees become productive, as well as protecting against adverse movements in price.

Training courses are provided for free, including accommodation. Nearly 5,000 farmers have attended the basic three-day course to date. Its alumni form a microcosm of the Philippines. Farmers from all corners of the archipelago have attended, some wearing their indigenous dress. Parish priests have taken part, looking to develop church-owned land to raise income. Mayors have sat in the classroom in the company of their armed bodyguards.

Besides on-site training, farmers are supported in the field by traveling agronomists. We met one of them, Prox Cortejos, along with his boss, Joel Lumagbas, as they visited one of

their coffee suppliers in Cavite. Paul and Tedd Belamide are a husband-and-wife team heading up a coffee farming and trading operation, growing their own and buying other farmers' output. Their interaction with Prox and Joel was familiar and relaxed, the latter's inputs clearly appreciated. "How much of your business is with Nescafé?" I asked. "All of it," Tedd answered, adding a smile, "Nescafé forever..."

After touring their farm, we were treated to *buko* juice, fresh off the tree. The business talk continued, with Joel talking about the pasture required to feed a carabao, against the market price for a liter of milk. He'll just as readily tell you the current market price of coffee and various intercropping products, the expected yield per intercropped hectare, and project your total revenues. Pio and Lionila Secadron, owners of a farm near Pangantukan in Bukidnon, used to extract 600 kilos of coffee per hectare. Following Prox's regular visits, they now regularly expect yields ranging from 2,000 to 3,000 kilos. Mario Ledesma runs Ragus Farm in Manolo Fortich, Bukidnon, close to the Del Monte pineapple plantation. Also visited by Prox, he is a diligent acquirer and applier of agricultural expertise. Walking around the farm, he peppers his conversation with terms like "beneficial weed," "companion plant" and "nitrogen fixer." Not surprisingly the berry clusters on his trees were particularly large.

This page and opposite: Planting time is approaching. Seedlings graduating from this nursery could be producing their first harvest in under two years.

Green beans in the sampling bin prior to grading: their quality will determine their price.

BRIDGING THE GAP

Typically, farmers sold their coffee to traders, who sold onto manufacturers. This system was low on transparency and high on risk. Sellers had to rely on information about market price and the quality of their coffee from a trader. If the farmer had no independent access to such information, he risked being underpaid. Direct buying was the approach chosen by Nescafé to address these issues. While coffee beans continue to be delivered to the Nestlé factory by farmers and traders, the first Nestlé satellite buying station opened in 1986 in Davao. Today, there are 11 buying stations throughout the country. Nestlé follows the world market price and communicates changes by SMS to its supplier farmers. Current prices are also posted visibly at the buying stations and announced on various radio stations. Grading criteria and methodology are published in pamphlets and also posted at the buying station. Once accepted and graded, the farmer is issued with a Receiving Report, which is as good as cash in hand. Within hours of issuing it, payment is issued at a local bank. Upon being shown the Receiving Report many local store owners, will allow farmers to do their shopping, and set it aside for cash payment and pickup later in the day.

The buying station we visited in Cavite was the sectioned-off area of a warehouse with a small glass-windowed office in the corner. Sacks of coffee were being unloaded. A metal probe was punched into each bag, extracting a coffee bean sample with a rasp, and dropped into a metal bin. One hundred grams were scooped out, and taken into the office. Through the window we saw a young woman hunched over the grading tray, identifying and counting defects. The rustle of the roaster was followed by the rattle of the grinder. Coffee was steeped in hot water, the liquid tasted with loud slurps. Another machine in the corner measured the moisture content of the beans. The results from sorting, tasting and moisture testing were all entered onto a quality-control sheet to determine the grade. The difference in price per kilo was less than 5% between grades 1 and 3. Grade rating times weight equals payment to the farmer.

I was curious. Farmers could manage defect content through careful sorting, but what about gauging moisture content? Ideally, beans need to have a moisture content below 12%. How can a farmer tell without an expensive machine? "Actually, they're pretty good at gauging humidity, even without a hydrometer," the station officer told me. "They have various ways of doing it," he continued. "Some grab half a fistful, shake it and listen to the sound the beans make as they strike each other. There is the grab and drop test: grab a fistful, then let go. The number of beans sticking to the palm is a measure of moisture content. The most popular is the bite test. Bite into a green bean. If it's chewy, it's too humid. The harder it is to bite into, the drier it is." I did not believe him. "OK, what do you think the humidity of this bean is?" He bit into it. "11%." He placed the sample in the hydrometer. The reading was 11.04%.

I spoke to one satisfied farmer in Cavite. I asked him what he liked about selling at the Nestlé satellite buying station. He moved his hand as if placing something on an imaginary tabletop. "Cash," he said simply. A few minutes later, he was holding a Receiving Report for 500,000 pesos.

This page and opposite bottom: probing the coffee sacks to test the beans.

Opposite top: Unloading and weighing the coffee bags.

The process of coffee cupping involves freshly roasted ground coffee being steeped in hot water after which the liquid is tasted in loud slurps.

Opposite (left to right): A grading tray is used to identify and count defects; and Filtering beans through the sampling can.

Freshly roasted coffee beans are raked to hasten the cooling process.

A HUMMING,
GIANT COFFEE MAKER

Things felt different as soon as we had made our way past the security station and stepped inside the compound of the Nescafé Cagayan de Oro plant. There seems to be precision and purpose everywhere you look, from the cut grass to the painted signs. Walls and rooflines seem to align and meet more neatly. A low audible hum pervades the air. People walk with a little more speed; no one ambles. There was efficiency in the use of space. One passageway was being used for an intramural aerobics class. There was faint smell of processing from the water recycling station. Hygiene was everywhere: hands were washed and caps worn over white gowns before entering production areas. External covered walkways connected buildings. There was no dust on them.

The walk through the coffee production areas of the plant is a succession of disproportionate sensations. Everything is on a bigger scale.

The forklift trucks have done their work for the day. The quiet warehouse smells of hemp sacks. We turn the corner, and start hearing a dry, sewing machine sound. It grows louder until you cannot converse anymore. Conveyor belts are rolling. The smell of hemp is a little more intense, mixed with dust. Men stand in twos on a row of giant hoppers, feeding coffee beans into them. It feels a little hotter. The beans are dried and moved into roasting. Drums the size of wet cement trucks lie on their sides. It's hot, but not humid. The aroma of roasted coffee floats on the heated air. The beans are in the cooling pond, and are being worked by revolving rakes. They've doubled in size and their noise when rubbing against each other is sharper, higher and hollow. The sound recedes and approaches all around us, like waves. After grinding the beans, the coffee is brewed. The nose breathes in the richly humid air. It could be a movie set for the engine room of a submarine. Dials, vats and suspended rails stand out among the engine noise, the sound of pumps at work, and the hiss of steam.

I can smell a giant cup of coffee. Finally, it is turned to powder. The pipes gurgle as the brewed coffee makes its way into drying. Now imagine that it has been raining, and that your clothes have been soaked through. You are standing at the top of a tower and looking down at a pile of hay below. You jump off. By the time you land, you are entirely dry. At the top you were liquid coffee; down below, you're soluble coffee powder.

Cupping: Tasting coffee made from roasted beans. A team effort to ensure quality.

Opposite: Small-batch coffee roasters used to produce tasting samples.

THE CHALLENGE OF SUCCESSION

Rudy Trillanes is the factory manager at Nescafé Cagayan de Oro. In 1973 he responded to a job advertisement for a "Food Manufacturing Company." He got the job at the original Nescafé factory in Alabang. He retires in 2008, when Nescafé celebrates its 70th anniversary. We only spent half a day at the Cagayan de Oro plant, and only part of it in his company. I've since developed a strong hunch that he is the source of a great deal of employee satisfaction there.

While interviewing him, I asked him which part of his job he had found to be the most fulfilling. Without hesitation, he talked of his work on the 1989 project team in charge of setting up a production plant in Dongguan, China. He was responsible for hiring and training individuals. Over the course of his four years there, he watched them grow. He has continued to do that since. He explained how he looked out for key signs that showed development in the people he coached. His greatest moments of professional satisfaction came when individuals began to work out problems for themselves, when they could act without instruction or script.

Growing up, his mother roasted her own coffee. He would roast and grind coffee too, but add his own touches. He described how he would roast beans with an eggshell to make the grinding easier. While roasting them he would choose the moment just before the beans cracked to add a little sugar. This made the beans stick to each other in clusters, and prevented

The finished product making its way through the packaging line.

spillage while working them through the corn grinder. He did not know it then, but his willingness to experiment with different approaches to fix problems showed a natural aptitude for production management.

Trillanes is also a senior vice-president within the corporate hierarchy. His bearing wore no signs of rank during our meeting. Later, while walking the factory floor with him, I saw that he wore his authority with ease, and that employees found him very approachable. He enjoys a sense of camaraderie. In the tasting room, the patter revolved around individual colleagues' expertise in coffee. One knew about coffee in the cup; the other, an agronomist, was an authority on green coffee. "Max can tell the blend of coffee in the cup with the first sip. With Mr. Santiago, you can throw a handful of green coffee at him, and he'll tell you which bean it is!" he delighted in telling us.

I challenged everyone to guess the moisture content of a sample of beans. He joined in the fun, and jumped up to find a piece of paper to write down everyone's guesses. He guessed 10.5%. I applied my expertise from Cavite and guessed 10. Titus said 9. The beans went into the hydrometer: 8.8%.

As we walked through the packaging lines, we took a shortcut through the truck receiving area to Trillanes' office. Just before walking outside, he handed us some fluorescent vests to wear.

It was the end of the day, and no trucks were being driven anymore. We walked the 20 meters to the back of his office across a quiet yard. As I took off my vest, I was impressed with his sense of compliance with safety rules, even for a low-risk walk across such a short stretch. I was wrong. As I shook his hand to say goodbye, I realized it was a sense of care. That is what his colleagues have been responding to.

An espresso machine at work. Precise
requirements and measures relating to grind,
packing density, temperature and exposure to
steam result in a cup fit for consumption.

Opposite (top to bottom): A long sequence of
work precedes this moment of enjoyment; and
Layers of flavor can be added to the beans. In
this case, hazelnut oil has been added to add
to the aroma of roasted coffee.

GLOBAL COFFEE TRENDS

by Henk Kwakman
Head of Coffee and Beverages Strategic Business Unit, Nestlé

Coffee is a sensorial and emotional pleasure. It is a catalyst to get you going in the morning. It can also give a moment of uplift, relaxation, indulgence or social connection. It can be the closure of a wonderful dinner with family or friends.

Coffee is a simple, accessible, affordable moment of pleasure in everyday life; and worldwide billions of people enjoy coffee every day.

In the last decade we have seen a global explosion of media communication and media access. Think about TV, mobile phones and Internet. Hand-in-hand with it came individualization. Better-educated and better-informed consumers who want to shape their own lifestyle and make their own choices. This has been combined with global economic progress and increasing time pressure. People now lead busier, more hectic and stressful lifestyles. The busier the day, the more those simple moments of coffee pleasure become important.

All those developments led to some key trends in coffee.

A trend towards better quality coffee.

A trend towards more choice in coffee. From coffee black/white/with or without sugar to coffee as a menu with espresso, cappuccino, latte, iced, decaf, etc.

A trend to more convenience. Single sticks of complete coffee mixes simplifying the preparation and also providing individual choice and bringing portability.

A trend towards coffee bars. Nice trendy places where people can escape the hectic pace of the city to sit down and have an enjoyable coffee experience at low cost.

Finally we see that health, nutrition and well-being play an increasingly important role for consumers when making a choice between brands and products. And this leads to the trend of coffee solutions with additional health benefits like antioxidants. Coffee is naturally very rich in antioxidants.

All of this leads to an enormous world coffee market. The annual coffee crop amounts to 7 billion kilos of green coffee. Calculated as cups of coffee, global consumption comes to more than 800 billion cups: billions of people enjoy coffee pleasure every day, and its consumption still grows every year.

If you multiply the number of cups with the price of a good cup of coffee, you start to understand that coffee is a global business employing millions of people both in agriculture and in industry.

Coffee beans at the market stall, glistening with aromatic oils brought out during the roasting process.

why we love coffee

Coffee powder, ground from lightly roasted beans. The darker the roast, the darker the shade of the bean, and the darker the powder.

Caffeine, adenosine and dopamine: these are three key terms in understanding the appeal of coffee. We all know caffeine. In pure form, it is an odorless white powder with a bitter taste.

Adenosine is a neurotransmitter created in the brain. Its levels build up each hour that we are awake, and increasing concentrations of it bring about sleepiness. Adenosine makes its presence felt by "binding" to adenosine receptors in the brain. As this happens, nerve cell activity slows down, causing drowsiness.

Think of adenosine as a messenger. It knocks on a door marked "adenosine receptor." The door opens exclusively to adenosine messengers. Once inside, the messenger delivers the message: Go to sleep. The longer the brain stays awake, the more messengers arrive, and the same message is delivered with increasing frequency until the nervous system goes into rest mode.

Caffeine poses as adenosine. It knocks on the same door. The door, thinking an adenosine messenger is knocking, opens up. Caffeine messenger enters and delivers its message: Wake up. Nerve cell activity speeds up. The pituitary gland senses the increased activity, and issues orders (releases hormones) for adrenaline production. Heartbeat rises, blood flow increases to muscles, breathing pipes open up. The liver releases sugar into the bloodstream for added energy. Muscles contract more easily.

Dopamine is another neurotransmitter that is associated with the "pleasure system" of the brain. It knocks on its own dedicated receptor doors, and delivers its message: You feel good. Dopamine is normally released by naturally rewarding experiences such as eating food. Caffeine stimulates production of dopamine. Unlike its conduct with adenosine, caffeine does not impersonate dopamine: it just arranges for more messengers to deliver their feel-good message.

Enhanced performance and pleasure: no wonder coffee is the second most traded commodity after oil.

Strictly business or budding romance: coffee does its work, whatever the context.

COFFEE — IT REALLY CAN BE GOOD FOR YOU

Caffeine makes its way into the bloodstream through the stomach. It is a quick journey: it can deliver its effects as quickly as 15 minutes after consumption. Once inside, it stays around for a while. It is estimated that caffeine exits the system six hours after entering it. This is why many coffee drinkers set 4:00 p.m. as the limit for drinking "leaded" coffee, choosing decaf after that time.

Coffee drinkers who feel they cannot start their day without a cup of coffee will often view their liking for it with varying levels of guilt. They might call their liking a need, maybe an addiction. Feelings about personal coffee consumption can be recast more positively. Over 19,000 studies have been conducted on the effects of coffee on health over the last few decades, and the findings are on the whole positive. While the medical community speaks of the need for more research, the firm consensus has built up in recent years that coffee does bring about health benefits.

Many benefits are preventive. Studies have shown that two cups of coffee a day can reduce the risk of colon cancer by 25%, of gallstones by 50% and of liver cirrhosis by 80%.[1]

Researchers at Harvard analyzed data from one study involving 126,000 people over 18 years, and calculated that one to three cups of coffee a day could reduce the onset of Type 2 diabetes by single digits. A dramatic reduction in risk occurred where individuals drank six cups or more a day. Men's risk went down by 54%, women's by 30% relative to non-coffee drinkers.

Vanderbilt University has an Institute for Coffee Studies. It conducts its own research and tracks studies worldwide. Some research findings indicate that coffee can counteract the effects of unhealthy habits such as heavy drinking and smoking. Apparently, heavy consumers of alcohol and users of nicotine who drink large amounts of coffee have lower incidences of heart disease and liver damage than their counterparts who don't drink it.

This page and opposite: Generations may differ in their experiences and tastes, but coffee manages to remain relevant to all.

Many studies indicate that regular coffee drinkers are up to 80% less likely to develop Parkinson's disease.[2] The beneficial substance in this case happens to be caffeine, and drugs are under development to treat Parkinson's disease that contain a derivative of caffeine.

There is also evidence that coffee may help alleviate asthma attacks when medication is unavailable.[3] This is due to caffeine's effect of opening up the breathing pipes.[4]

Researchers in Italy have identified trigonelline, a compound that gives coffee its aroma and bitter taste, as having antibacterial and anti-adhesive properties that can keep dental cavities from forming.

An added advantage to bear in mind is that coffee is a rich source of antioxidants. As their name indicates, antioxidants are substances that can counteract the natural but damaging process of oxidation in animal tissue. Oxidation is what causes oil to become rancid, iron to rust and peeled apples to turn brown. The same process of oxidation within the body can damage cells, proteins and DNA. Harmful molecules called free radicals are to blame, and antioxidants can neutralize them. As we age, cell parts damaged by oxidation accumulate. Antioxidants are believed to play a role in preventing the development of degenerative diseases. They do this by preventing cell damage caused by oxidation.

Caffeine is a substance also often used in cosmetic creams — especially slimming creams — where it is credited with toning and conditioning skin. There are exceptions to health benefits resulting from coffee. Excess consumption can bring on hand trembling and nervousness, but studies show no significant adverse effects on healthy people consuming up to six cups a day.

Notes/References:
(1) *The Buzz on Coffee, The latest research shows your morning pick-me-up may be brimming with health benefits.* WebMD Medical News, www.webmd.com. Kathleen Zelman, MPH, RD/LD.
(2) *Caffeine Fuels Most Energy Drinks.* WebMD Medical News, www.webmd.com. Tomas DePaulis, PhD, research scientist, Vanderbilt University's Institute for Coffee Studies; research assistant professor of psychiatry, Vanderbilt University Medical Center, Nashville.
(3) *The effects of low doses of caffeine on human performance and mood.* Psychopharmacology, 92, 308-312. Liska, K. (1986).
(4) *Caffeine use and young adult women.* Journal of Drug Education, 12, 273-283. Victor, B. S., Lubetsky, M., & Greden, J. F. (1981).

Over 19,000 studies have been conducted on the effects of coffee on health over the last few decades, and the findings are on the whole positive.

coffee recollections

Coffee at Café Cabalen: Setting can enhance the enjoyment of coffee.

*"I have measured out my life
in coffee spoons."*

-T.S. Eliot

Coffee has become so embedded in daily life that it hardly stands out on its own. People rarely remember coffee as a single event, but as a long-standing personal habit or a group tradition. In researching material for this book, we found that coffee emerged as a regular activity conducted over lengths of time, associated with a phase or chapter of one's life. UP alumni recall drinking coffee in the Basement Cafeteria. Childhood memories are framed by regular family gatherings around the coffee pot. That coffee shop in the corner is where colleagues used to go for a break. It is an accessory activity, the bass guitar in the band. It is the exceptions that make coffee memorable on its own.

A friend's father went through a prolonged period of depression. During those years, she remembers sitting at the kitchen table listening to her mother talk about her worries. She can still see her mother's head looking down, a hand wrapped around a cup of coffee, as if hanging on to a reassuring prop.

The first Figaro coffee shop opened in 1993, kicking off the national café trend. Several chains followed, and there are now over 200 coffee shops in Metro Manila. They provided new opportunities for socializing, and new venues for dating in particular. Coffee has been found to offer a low-key, flexible introduction: a cup can be drawn out as long as pleasantly possible or cut short as needs dictate. If things go well, there will be more coffee dates, eventually an escalation in commitment to lunch or dinner. If things go further, there'll be a meal with the family. And so on. There are many events in a relationship's history that a boyfriend may have forgotten, but chances are he'll remember that first coffee meeting.

At Panciteria Lido, siphon coffee jugs transform water into dark liquid. This dark liquid is the full strength coffee patrons enjoy.

BINONDO HAVEN
COFFEE IN LIFE, AND BEYOND DEATH

Most visitors enter Binondo from the south, passing a row of Manila landmarks along the way. Rizal Park, the Manila Hotel, City Hall, Intramuros, the disused Metropolitan Theatre; up ahead, the Jones Bridge over the Pasig River. As often happens with bridges, the changes on the far shore are abrupt. Leaving wide-open spaces behind, the car enters into a warren of streets. The sky becomes scarce, cars have less space to share; the narrow shop fronts and doorways file past in dense succession. A new set of landmarks begins. Straight ahead is Binondo Church, its octagonal 16th-century tower rising pagoda-like, its red brickwork exposed, to a domed roof. A sharp right takes you into Ongpin Street, past the Eng Bee Tin store. If the purple fire truck is parked in front, it's a cheerful sight: no buildings are on fire, and thoughts turn to Chua's famed *ube hopia*. Should we buy some on the way home? A little later, a left turn leads into T. Alonzo. Eyes turn left, scanning for the sign. There it is. Up some stairs, and we enter Panciteria Lido.

The décor is light cream Formica, the lighting neon-white; the seats are metal and vinyl. The owner, gray-haired Mr. King, surveys the scene from the door. Opposite him, high on the wall and flanked by red candles, is a statue of Tu Di Gong, whose worshippers often address him as grandfather. It is April, and Christmas decorations and greetings hang on the walls.

We take our seats, and spot the siphon coffee pots. The conversation stops as heads turn to the counter to watch the coffee boys at work. They tend a row of double-balloon pots, and watch as heated water rises from the lower glass spheres and turns into coffee in the upper jugs. As the water below runs out, the gas flames are turned off, and the dark liquid above

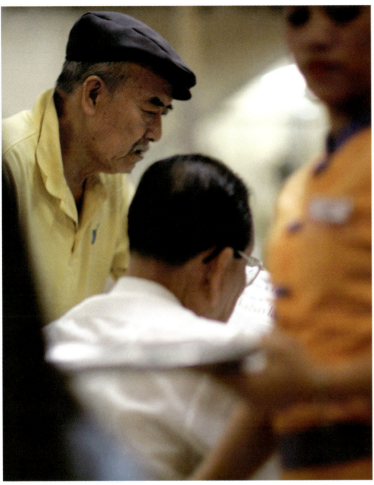

flows through the grinds once more into the jugs below, where it gathers as full strength coffee. Table pots are filled, jugs washed and readied for the next batch. We sip appreciatively.

Left to right: Coffee being poured for a customer. On average, this happens 800 times a day; Coffee grounds swirling in hot water: the moment before these are filtered out in the downward rush of coffee, ready for serving; and greetings, stories, gossip, details — the stuff of community and conviviality.

Most customers are elderly gentlemen sitting quietly on their own. Some lean forward, absorbed in Chinese newspapers, but most sit upright, facing the television sets in the corners. A little observation confirms that they hardly look at the screens. Instead, their eyes travel discretely, taking in the detail around them, clocking the new faces at the other table or gazing off in distant concentration. Senator Alfredo Lim is at his usual table. My granddaughter told me about that actress sitting in the corner. What was her name again? Ah yes, it was Gretchen Barreto. Is that Harry Ongpin? Must be an important meeting. Recollections and reflections are occasionally interrupted to shake hands with a friend, or talk to one of the young waitresses. These are clad in pale orange uniforms and bustle about between tables and counters. When not loading trays, sending in food orders or clearing dishes they stand about in twos and threes, chatting quietly. All of a sudden, an alarmed whoop. It appears that one of the customers felt a temptation while walking back to his table, and yielded to it. Did he say something indiscreet, or was it a pinch? The aggrieved waitress shifts into scolding mode. She marches up to the offender and slaps him on the arm. The guilty party recoils from the punishment. Was that a mischievous glint in his eye? Her colleagues giggle noisily.

Managing the staff is the job of Corin, a 15-year veteran at Panciteria Lido, whose style is equal parts firm hand and kind smile. She combines a sense of duty with a fondness for her customers, and is many a regular's favorite for sharing his family stories. Their children moved into far-off neighborhoods and subdivisions a long time ago, and Lido has become their second home. Some die-hard regulars are so keen to start their day that they'll be found knocking on the doors at 5:30 in the morning. When let in before opening time they will help with setting up: turning on the lights, starting the air conditioning and flicking the switches on the water heater. One wheelchair-bound customer is regularly carried up and down the stairs by the coffee boys.

Nature will take its course, and sooner or later one of their regular customers passes away. Lido's contact endures beyond death. Corin will arrange for coffee to be delivered to the funeral parlor as an offering, prepared the way the deceased used to enjoy it. At one family's request coffee was served at the former customer's regular table for three days. They wanted to make sure their loved one enjoyed his time before departing the land of the living for good.

It does not take long for the place to grow on you. It is not the first impression upon entering that stays with you, but the enjoyable aftertaste that lingers. A pleasing and reassuring pattern has formed itself by the time you finish your first pot of coffee. Quiet customers, rushing waitresses and busy coffee boys, the ebb and flow of their motions set by the upward rush of water, and the downward flow of coffee.

Interviewing Corin at Panciteria Lido for the book was an exercise in being charmed, assured and impressed in the course of half an hour. She sits upright in her chair. Her hair is combed into place precisely, and somehow you know that she ironed her immaculate blouse herself. You wouldn't guess that it takes her one and a half hour's commuting on public transportation — with its open windows and dusty roads — to get to work. Confidence blends with the eagerness to please. Her sense of dignity flows from her employers' appreciation for her work, and her knowledge of what it takes to do the job well. Not a single negative sentiment is expressed during our interview. Details about Panciteria Lido's history, ownership and clientele are provided quickly. The interview could end there and then, but we want to spend more time with her, and find out more about her. To draw out the interview, we stray into asking personal questions. "How long have you been working here?"; "Where did you work before?"; "Do you enjoy working here?" Each answer is accompanied by a polite nod and a shy smile. Finally, we ask the most intimate question. We want to know what marks her working day. "What do you have for breakfast?" Her eyes brighten a little more, the smile is a little broader. She bounces lightly in her chair, recalling the enjoyment at the start of her day. "Garlic rice," she tells us enthusiastically. And coffee? "Oh yes, Nescafé."

Left: A blue flame goes to work on a clear jug — another coffee brewing cycle begins.

Right: Corin, Head Waitress. Equal parts kind smile and firm hand.

SAVING FIRST IMPRESSIONS

"You only get one shot at making a first impression." These words from Lola Hilda, his grandmother's sister, had been ringing in Jose Cruz's head with increasing regularity lately. He was about to turn 25 and was going to graduate from his master's program in a few weeks. He was interviewing for jobs, and he was also about to announce his engagement to Tina.

The phone rang. It was a prospective employer, one of the most prestigious financial services companies in Makati. Jose had gone through two rounds of interviews, and already had a date for the third and final round. The recruiter apologized, but one vice president he had been scheduled to meet with needed to rearrange his calendar. Would he be able to come a day earlier, at 2:00 p.m.? "Of course," he responded immediately, "14th February, 2:00 p.m. I'll see you then. Thank you!" He put the phone down. He repeated the date and time a few times, sensing that there was something else to bear in mind. He murmured to himself as he opened his calendar. 14th February, 7:00 p.m., Valle Verde — and framed in multiple lines of red pen: Announcement. OK, panic over. He did not double-book, but it was going to be a tight schedule: he would have to go from Makati directly to Tina's parents to announce their engagement. *Corny naman* she chose Valentine's Day to do it. Oops. Mustn't say that out loud anymore.

The Big Day arrived. He'd been late getting his suit from the dry cleaner at the mall. Better to eat there than risk not eating anything at all. He dashed into the food court, spotted the smallest line, got his dish, wolfed it down. Home for a quick shower, into the suit, and off to the interview. As he drove down EDSA, he began to savor the aftertaste of lunch. It was pure garlic. Lola Hilda's alarm bell went off. Damn, I'll be talking with garlic on my breath to someone who's deciding whether or not to give me a job! He parked the car, walked into the building and ran into his classmate Joey, also interviewing. "What's up Jose, you look really stressed. This isn't like you..." Before Joey could finish, Jose had explained the situation. Joey agreed it was a problem. Some quick thinking was needed. "I know. Follow me." He went into the company's self-service canteen. "Here — take these," handing him a few stick sachets of instant coffee. "What,..." Jose started. "Empty those into your mouth. That will take the garlic breath away." With five minutes to go before his appointment, Jose rushed into the washrooms and did as told. The taste was overwhelming, but it was for a good cause.

On the way to Valle Verde he performed another coffee mouth rinse.

He had just returned from his honeymoon and was spending the first night in his new home. He was putting the finishing touches to a proposal for a new client. Tina walked out of the bathroom and into his study, looking puzzled. "Honey, why is there a jar of Nescafé next to the toothpaste?"

He swears he is never as witty as this
without coffee. She agrees.

DURIAN AND COFFEE:
DOUBLE-BARRELLED SATISFACTION

Amadeo, Cavite, is thought of as the coffee capital of the Philippines. It actually ranks fourth in national production. First through third and fifth place all go to Mindanao provinces: Sultan Kudarat, Compostela Valley, Davao City and Davao del Sur. Batangas, the cradle of Philippine coffee production, ranks 13th. This makes Mindanao the nation's top producer, accounting for nearly three quarters of total coffee output. Durian is synonymous with Davao, and it was only a matter of time before the two came together.

My introduction to durian was memorable. It took place outside the Philippines through the arrangements of a Malaysian friend of the family. She had taken a shine to myself and my wife, and was always introducing us to new food experiences. She was enthusiastic about giving us a taste of durian. Many a stranger to the fruit has commented on its smell; we will not add to it here. Eating it is a series of strong sensations of the nose, palate and mouth. Scientifically speaking, the fruit has 43 sulfur-containing compounds. One of these is hydrogen sulfide, which occurs in rotten eggs. Another is diethyl sulfide, found in aging meat. But keeping them company are two other kinds of smell: one delicate and fruity, the other strong and onion-like. Durian has a

heavy, creamy, custard-like consistency. Sugar, musk and smoke sensations trade places. Some think of gasoline, smoked fish, or both. It lays down a trail of heat as it travels down the esophagus. Our friend, a matronly figure, moaned with each mouthful.

Davao's Blugré Coffee has pulled off a pleasing combination of durian with coffee. The Durian Gatchpuccino — named after Gatchi Gatchalian, Blugré's owner — is a remarkably successful mix of the two. The drink commands attention with each sip, making the palate sit up and pay attention. Firm, well-defined flavors hang on an elaborate structure of sensations. The durian is present in all its complexity, without being overwhelming. The milk complements the fruit's creaminess. The heat of the liquid echoes the chemical heat of the fruit. The taste of coffee manages to hold its own throughout. The secret appears to be in the carefully calibrated proportion of liquid to fruit: enough to dilute the concentration of flavor, but not too much to diminish it. To the uninitiated, it is a great introduction to durian. It provides a measured experience of the fruit, with caffeine thrown in. Fans of both durian and coffee must love the double helpings of dopamine that come from drinking it.

ABOUT BANANAS AND COFFEE

Bananas can claim equal prominence with the durian in Davao: these provide the defining theme at Kasagingán Kapehan on Torres Street. Its logo is a high-stepping banana skin balancing a cup of coffee — a cross of can-can girl and band majorette. The owners' inspiration for the idea was drawn from family tradition. As far back as Benjie Lizada and his sister Amy Lou can remember, coffee was always served with a banana dish in their parents' and grandparents' households. They decided to prolong and expand the tradition in a business. The banana-coffee combination is the bananapuccino, a pleasing blend of coffee and extract of banana. As with its durian counterpart, the banana flavor finds a ready complement in the creaminess of the milk. Both are held together by coffee and caffeine. Amy Lou's culinary expertise — honed at annual cooking school retreats — is evident throughout the menu. Classic Pinoy merienda fare is refined and presented with a twist, sometimes with a witty name. *Maruya* becomes *Mmmaruya Supreme*, dressed with a thick thread of rich chocolate and served in an elegant arrangement. *Turon* becomes *tworon*. Banana Crumble, Banana Luck and Banana Dream Pie are additional theme favorites, and more are under development.

Top: Coffee and milk, when skillfully blended, can actually tame the relative excesses of the spiky durian.
Bottom: In the Philippines, banana is an old friend and well matched companion to coffee.

PHILIPPINE FAMILY ACQUIRES DUTCH SON

As Nestlé's Zone Director for Asia, Oceania, Africa and Middle East, Frits van Dijk keeps in regular touch with the Philippines. He was based in Manila during the seventies and again in the eighties, and recalls his time in the country with great fondness. He is a Dutch national born in Jakarta, on the island where coffee was first cultivated in the 17th century. At his family's various homes away from the Netherlands he was reared on the Dutch value of *gezelligheid*. It is a word that stands for nearness, closeness, conviviality: comforting, cozy and sheltering, both in physical space and personal relations. It is the aim of gatherings with friends and family over meals and drinks.

He first came to the Philippines in 1975 from a posting in India. He was immediately struck by the Philippines' own expression of *gezelligheid*. He recalls fondly the ready hospitality that he received as a stranger wherever he went. His hosts were always attentive to his well-being and comfort, yet relaxed and uncomplicated in their manner. It was a reassuring start to his time in the country. It was not long before he was also impressed. He noticed that the desire to nurture family ties and friendships ran stronger here than elsewhere he had been to. Family events were held with greater frequency, and each opportunity to get together pursued with great intensity.

Working in an archipelago was also a new experience. Distributing product across 60 distribution centers - exceptional within any national market - and a large part of it by boat, provided valuable learning and insight. Having to live with the risk of typhoons and their potential for interrupting operations was also new. He recalls a business trip in Northern Mindanao where a bridge had collapsed, and had to consider driving into the river to cross it. He observed how trucks and jeepneys forded the water slowly but without difficulty, and decided it was safe for him to do so. He got into his car and drove in. The first few meters went fine, but then he realized that he had not made allowance for the car he was driving. His Volkswagen Beetle, with smaller wheels and reduced weight, began to lose traction on the river bed, and began to float.

He did eventually cross the river, even if further downstream from the other cars. The fright over, he observed that he had just learned something new: that an adventure is defined by an experience that is not enjoyed while it is happening. He was in his twenties, living adventures and getting paid for it. Life could not get much better than this. It did get even better, but more on that later.

In 1985 he returned to the Philippines as Marketing Director. In February 1986 he collected another exceptional memory. He counts himself fortunate for having witnessed extraordinary history at first hand. Beyond the magnitude of the EDSA Revolution, he was also impressed by the Philippine talent for improvisation. Supply lines came into being spontaneously, carrying food and drink deep into the crowds. Even hot coffee was available first thing in the morning.

There were other professional and personal milestones in the Philippines. Nescafé's diamond jar was launched under his management. Little did he know at the time that it would become a production prop for the national film industry. His most memorable and enduring friendship began at the Hyatt Hotel in Baguio in 1976. Many meetings over coffee followed. In August 2007 he celebrated his 30th wedding anniversary with his wife, Jeng Castro van Dijk, and their two children.

It is when we see ourselves in others, and they see themselves in us, that relations are formed. Differences based on nationality fall away, and bonds are forged from an awareness of shared humanity. When he got married, his wife got him a special present. A jeepney was too big, but she found something just as

Coffee sprouts

representative of the Philippines, and easier to transport. It is to be found parked in the living room of his home in Switzerland: an ice cream cart. A dirty ice cream cart? "Yes, a dirty ice cream cart!" he replied, roaring with laughter. The author proposes to confer on him the title of Honorary Filipino.

Café by the Ruins, Baguio: A setting that manages to be both rustic and elegant, with an equally imaginative kitchen.

Opposite: Breakfast room service, Manila Hotel. Delicately sliced mango and coffee are de rigueur.

Dom Myron checking the coffee tree on the grounds of the Monastery of the Transfiguration, Malaybalay, Bukidnon.

TOWARDS A CUP OF TRANQUIL COFFEE

Andrew Lui was praying for his working day to end soon. The purchasing manager of one of his largest clients, a prominent convent school in Davao, was sitting in front of him. There had been an unfortunate mistake in the last delivery of stationery supplies, and he was being made to do penance for it. It was very unsettling to have a nun look at him in anger. God's wrath was rumbling nearby.

He was glad to meet a friend for dinner that evening. Professional discomfiture faded as the evening went on. Easy banter and stories were swapped. Over coffee his friend started to tell him about her time as a preschool teacher in Malaybalay. She looked at her cup. "You know, there's a monastery there where they produce their own coffee. It's great to visit. They host a brunch every second Sunday of the month, and all are welcome. The monks are really nice." A short pause. "Wait, what day is today? Hey, there's one tomorrow!" Another pause, while she looked at her watch and calculated, eyes locked on a distant object. "Andrew, let's go! We can take the midnight bus!"

Andrew's earlier moment of stress flashed by. He had a business to run. He couldn't just take off like that. He really needed a restful night's sleep, specially today. Monasteries are not cool. Quick, he had to shut this down. He summoned nonchalance and authority into his voice. "You're crazy. Malaybalay is a five-hour drive away."

He could not decide if it was shock or disbelief that accompanied him as the bus drove north through the outskirts of Davao. How had she done it? It was that look, a mix of girlish charm and boyish gamesmanship; gentle pleading, and a promise to insult his sense of manhood. Now he needed to make the most of it. He could sleep getting there. As the bus entered the open country, the speed increased. So did the number of curves, and of hills. The driver shifted into racing mode, and the bus threw itself violently from side to side.

It was then he smelled the ripe durian in the front row, and an intense craving for the fruit kicked in. Happy yet aching

Andrew Lui, after his restorative monastery brunch. He resolves to return and maybe one day live in Malaybalay.

Opposite: Dried coffee cherries arranged in rows.

At the monastery, testing the aroma of green beans is part of the process of producing coffee.

associations rushed into his mind. Abruptly, they were crowded out by the smell of cigarette smoke. Earlier discomforts had been enough. That cigarette was going to be put out or move far away. "No ifs or butts." The man behind looked up in mild surprise as Andrew turned to face him. Andrew looked down, his surprise a little greater as he saw, pointing toward the ceiling, the muzzle of a very large gun, and a large expanse of uniform behind it. Andrew became a passive smoker. Sleepless hours dragged on in the discomfort of the ride, heightened by the longing for durian, the smell of smoke and the fear of a gun.

It was 5:30 am when the bus finally stopped in Malaybalay. Stiff limbs tumbled out of the bus into the gray light of a hushed town. Eyes blinked away their sleep, and traveled upwards to

the hills, where mist moved slowly between the trees. The air felt cool, and carried the cleansing scent of pine. Slowly, each breath became more invigorating, the ears more alert. Old pine needles crunched pleasantly underfoot. The only traffic noise was a quiet hum behind the horizon. The sun began to spill into the valley. The scene above shone bright and golden. Crisp, thrilling detail came to the fore. A cock crowed in celebration, the hearty sound arching high into the sky. There was a bounce in his step as Andrew went in search of coffee at the Monastery of the Transfiguration.

Mass was held in the Locsin-designed chapel, and seemed longer than usual. Overlooking the altar was a seated black Madonna and Child, a replica of the statue of Our Lady of Montserrat in the founding Benedictine monastery in Spain. Saint Ignatius had prayed in front of the original in 1522. It was the turning point of his life that led to the creation of the Society of Jesus a decade and a half later.

Andrew's second wind was winding down. At 9 o'clock guests took their seats in the outdoor dining area, looking out onto cornfields and the chapel. Most were in their Sunday best, and Andrew and friend hoped that their worn-all-night chic would not stand out.

The monastery's coffee was poured. The first cup went down unnoticed. Bananas, Cagayan-style *kinilaw* with *suha* and *gatá*, pork *adobo* followed. The caffeine started to do its work. With his senses revived, he started on a second cup. Yes, the trip had been worth it for the coffee alone. A satisfying mouthful of Arabica taste, its dark roast aromas filling the mouth, but kept in check with Robusta flavors: like a fruity red wine with a strong backbone of tannins. It was a strong cup, tipping to the voluptuous side of well-balanced. The coffee made Andrew relaxed and aware, and he began to look around. The evident care taken in roasting and blending the coffee was mirrored all around. The Benedictine ethos of *ora et labora* was there in the neatness of the buildings, fields and driveways, and in the monks' attention to detail in preparing the dishes and arranging furniture and fittings. The monthly brunch is one of the few times the monks are allowed to relax their vow of silence, and they chatted eagerly with family and strangers alike. *Ginataan* joined the table. Cup followed cup,

and before long Andrew was becoming friends with the monks. Their sense of serenity became very appealing to an angst-ridden 25-year old, and Andrew divined that he had something valuable to learn from them.

Historians believe that the first organized cultivation of coffee plants took place in Sufi monasteries in the Yemen, where it was used to ensure alertness during night-time prayers. The first one of these might have been in Mocha. Monk's Blend provides an income to the Monastery of the Transfiguration, and it is somehow fitting that coffee should find a new monastic purpose a thousand years on. The Monastery finds itself as the keeper of several connections. It is a Philippine brotherhood whose origins lie in the work of Spanish monks. Its cultivation of coffee, in a contemporary Christian institution, has a precedent in medieval Islam. And last but not least, a link between two religious orders. The land on which this Benedictine monastery stands was donated by Bishop Francisco Claver, S.J. It might have been a small gesture of thanks for hosting Saint Ignatius in Montserrat in 1522.

Andrew resolved to return, and maybe one day live in Malaybalay. He now thinks monasteries with coffee are very appealing.

An Igorot house in Sagada, surrounded with sweet potato plants and coffee trees in its backyard.

COFFEE IN HIGH PLACES

Sagada, for its size, has an exceptional concentration of attractions. The limestone landscape is a pine-covered tumble of ridges and gullies. Underground streams carve out caves and feed fields. There are rice terraces here too, in Barangay Fidelisan. They are not as famous as the ones in Banaue, but no less appealing. The Banaue rice terraces overwhelm with their massive scale and verticality: they are the steps on which the god Lomawig descended to earth to enlighten the Igorot people. The Sagada terraces are of more intimate proportions. They do not climb to the sky, and individually rarely rise more than a foot or two in height. Their neatness of line speaks of great precision, and an appreciation of what the land can yield when handled with care. When the rice is tall, the paddies turn into a pleasing quilt of bright - green velvet patches, their stems nodding in waves to the passing breeze. It is next to these that you find the coffee trees, and one is hard pressed to imagine them in better company.

Karst cliffs rise out of the ground closer to the town of Sagada. They wear the "hanging coffins" for which the place is famous. The sight of them prompts hushed respect from the visitor, and an awareness of Kankana-ey presence, tradition and spirituality. They must have greeted the arrival of one Jaime Masferré in 1896.

He had just left the Spanish infantry in nearby Bontoc to join fellow ex-soldiers Moldero and Villaverde, who had started a farm on a 100 hectare homestead in Balatao, some 2 km from town. It was the start of coffee cultivation in Sagada. Moldero and Villaverde soon departed, leaving the farm to Masferré. In 1904 the Rev. John Staunton of the Episcopal Church of America visited Sagada and stayed at Masferré's farm. Staunton appreciated Masferré's hospitality, and came to rely on him as a translator in his first contacts with his future flock. He also commented in letters to friends and colleagues on the excellence of Masferré's coffee. It was the start of an association that continues to make its mark today.

Sagada's altitude makes it ideal for the growing of Arabica coffee, and the quality of the beans must have made its cultivation in such a remote place worthwhile. In Masferré's time the coffee was transported on horseback along trails to Cervantes to the southwest, over the Bessang Pass and onto Tagudin, where it was sold to Spanish merchants. It is thought that the original coffee seed came to Sagada from Batangas, and it was a matter of time before the coffee blight traveled north and caught up with Masferré's trees, wiping out the plantation. Staunton employed

110 kapihan

Sagada rice terraces. Coffee can be found among the rice fields, and on hillsides.

Opposite: Backyard coffee tree at Sagada. This one provides the family's needs.

him at the Mission, and appointed him as a lay missionary by 1909. Masferré was also in charge of the Mission Office, handling the administration of a medical dispensary, church and school. The last two of these remain to this day.

Staunton was the celebrant of Jaime Masferré's marriage to Mercedes Konyap, of Kankana-ey descent. Of their eight children, one, Albert, was ordained into the Episcopal priesthood. Another, Eduardo, taught himself photography and became the celebrated chronicler of Igorot life and custom. Eduardo's son Pancho today owns the Masferré Inn. It is a popular place for meals, and one of the most pleasant experiences in Sagada is to sit in the log-cabin style dining room by the windows, sipping a cup of coffee while looking across the Episcopal Church on the far ridge.

Half a century after Staunton's arrival, the Episcopal Church brought another prominent figure to Sagada. Anthropologists like to tell a joke among themselves. "How many anthropologists does it take to change a light bulb?" "One, but he has to live with it for at least a year." William Henry Scott lived here until the end of his days. In the words of one epitaph, he "was born an American, but died an Igorot." A respected historian on the Cordilleras and the prehispanic period, he is best known for his book The Discovery of the Igorots. He is affectionately remembered as Scotty, and his work is credited with bringing about a celebration of, and respect for, Igorot culture.

Pine trees covering the hills in and around Sagada. The altitude is ideal for growing Arabica variety beans.

Coffee trees grow wild in between homes in Sagada.

Villia Jefremovas arrived in 1979. She is now a professor of anthropology, and has made Sagada her home. Her house is perched on the edge of Echo Valley, and she counts the days she spends away from it. When she first arrived those who could afford it drank Nescafé while others drank brewed coffee from locally grown beans, often from their backyards. Having acquired a taste for Italian espresso while growing up, she sought out roasted beans. Happily, this impressed the locals: her taste for brewed coffee earned her a reputation for modesty, a quality much admired by Igorots. Roasted coffee was hard to come by though, and eventually a friend offered to have her mother roast it in neighboring Besao. The raw beans traveled there by bus, where they were roasted in a clay pot over a wood fire and pounded, then made their way back the following day. She recently added a small electric coffee roaster to her restaurant-grade kitchen. And just in case the power fails, she keeps a hand-powered coffee grinder at hand. Her acceptance into the Igorot community came quickly enough. She, her husband and daughter were given Igorot names, and her spouse was invited into the elders' council.

It was while visiting her home that we met someone who had made Sagada his home. He had left his home town in Europe in 1992, leaving behind a lucrative but demanding job as a top chef.

He was a burned-out shell of a man. He mounted his bicycle and headed east. Eight years and 50,000 km later he arrived in Sagada. He has seen more places than most, and he has not left. In time, he too was given an Igorot name.

At the time of writing, the road imposed a five-hour drive from Baguio. Two hours of paved surface to Mt. Data gave way to three hours of rough terrain. It is a hard-earned arrival, but the visitor soon realizes that the difficulty of getting there keeps Sagada from being overrun, and preserves its charm. The return drive to Baguio started in the afternoon. The road led into and out of clouds that were rushing over mountaintops and filtering the setting sun. Here and there the outline of a steep slope came into view, a lone pine on its edge standing guard. It was an image that would have drawn the attention of the Japanese woodblock artist Ando Hiroshige, and a fitting seal on the journey. May Sagada remain inaccessible except to the most appreciative visitors.

Dried and husked Arabica beans, ready for roasting.

Opposite: Coffee trees grow on slopes while flat surfaces are kept for rice in Sagada.

CORDILLERA ROASTING, TOASTING AND CUPPING

While photographing coffee trees and workers in Aguid, Sagada, Neal Oshima (this book's photographer), met Joseph Gonggeng, a widower in his mid-sixties. Joseph is a rice farmer, and has also been tending a ravine's worth of coffee trees for four years, continuing a tradition that has been in his family for generations. His father gave him a coffee-roasting *palayok*, which he still uses today. Neal promptly became a customer, and Joseph roasted a batch of green beans on the spot. Turning the *palayok* on its side over a wood fire, he moved and stirred the beans over the heat for about half an hour. Neal heard a first, and then a second crack as the beans expanded with the heat. Unlike industrial roasters who heed these sounds, Joseph paid more attention to the way the beans looked. Once he judged them properly roasted, he tossed them onto a rattan basket for cooling. A meat grinder was put to work. It was a very dark roast, which seems to reflect the local taste for coffee.

Afterward Neal's guide Dailay offered a gift of green coffee. While picking it up from his home, he also offered samples of home-made persimmon and pear wines. Comments were exchanged over the concentrated sweetness of the persimmon, and the pleasing sourness of the pear. Dailay produces these as a

sideline, and his ambitions are to expand into coffee. He reckons that the flesh of the coffee cherry contains the right amount of sugar for making wine. The side-by-side accompaniment of coffee by alcohol is an old favorite in European cafés, and having alcohol and caffeine deliver their respective effects in the same drink would be a novel experience. Neal thought of cold medicine for a while now he can't wait for that first toast.

Meat grinders grind coffee too — the resulting grind, a particularly dark roast.

Opposite: Joseph Gonggeng, roasting coffee in his palayok.

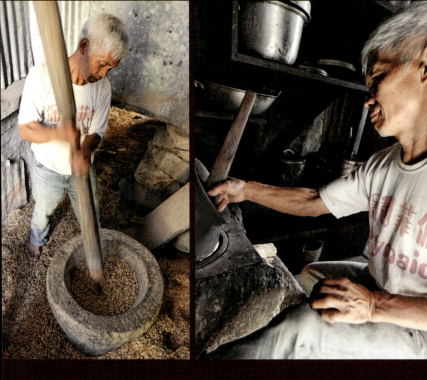

*From growing to harvesting to drying,
husking, and roasting,... Joseph Gonggeng
is the original coffee expert.*

Spontaneous hospitality during the rice harvest in Kalinga. We were taking a roadside break when these steaming cups of coffee were brought to us.

Opposite: Joseph Gonggeng walks through his coffee forest in search of coffee berries.

Following the Chico River north leads into Kalinga Province. While traveling there Neal got a glimpse of how coffee might have grown wild in the forests of Ethiopia before it was farmed. Centuries-old acacia trees adorned with ferns, orchids and epiphytes stood guard, canopies offering shade and shelter over a stand of mature Robusta trees. In Danguy, Lubuagan — a few kilometers from Mountain Province — Neal asked the driver, Clester, to stop at a roadside photo opportunity. Field workers were drying newly harvested rice in the morning sun. Conversation soon flowed over the pros and cons of traditional heirloom and newer hybrid varieties of rice. Neal quickly became busy, focusing on the details and framing of his compositions, becoming more and more absorbed in his work. Then, as he turned around and looked up, he and Clester were offered steaming cups of Kalinga coffee. It was freshly brewed from freshly roasted beans. Spontaneous hospitality is the most memorable.

Old Acacia trees, over 100 years old, sheltering coffee trees.

Coffee has endless possibilities. Coffee stain artwork by child prodigy CJ De Silva.

more than just black and white

Searing according to the Blackened Fish recipe. The rubbed-on seasoning includes coffee granules.

Chef Instructor Jam Mendoza of American Hospitality Academy.

RECIPES

These recipes were created exclusively for this publication by Chef Gene Cordova, President and Managing Partner of American Hospitality Academy Philippines and Chef Jam Mendoza. It is a collection that runs the spectrum from savoury to sweet, main course to dessert and *merienda*. The serious food enthusiast will find in them proof of Cordova's training at Le Cordon Bleu and Ecole de Ritz, as well as of his love for Philippine cooking. Enjoy the ingenious amalgamations of coffee into classic recipes and established favorites.

COFFEE ADOBO

The coffee appears in two components: in the crispy *adobo* flakes, and in the cream cheese. The *soy-and-suka* flavor of classic *adobo* is tempered with cream, and prepares the ground for the coffee flavors. This dish is a tremendously original reworking of an old favorite. Think of a golden oldie song that has been reworked with a new beat, and becomes a chartbuster. Knowing this dish could lead to many a craving. This is another candidate for the List of Favorite Comfort Food Dishes.

Makes 30 puff pastries

For the adobo shreds
2 tablespoons vegetable oil
500 grams of pork *kasim*, large cut
6 cloves of garlic, crushed
5 tablespoons soy sauce
black peppercorns, to taste
1 piece bay leaf
2 tablespoons vinegar
4 teaspoons cream
2 teaspoons instant coffee powder
vegetable oil, for frying

For the coffee cream cheese
1 pack of cream cheese, softened
instant coffee powder, to taste

Puff pastry

1. To prepare 1 day in advance: Put oil in a pan and lightly brown pork. Add garlic then sauté. Add soy sauce, peppercorn and bay leaf, then bring to a simmer. Add 1 cup of water and bring to a boil. Bring down to a simmer and leave on heat until meat is almost tender. Once tender, increase heat and add vinegar. Once the sauce thickens, add cream and coffee. Cool mixture and put in the chiller overnight to increase flavor.

2. The day after: Separate pork from the sauce and shred the pork. Set aside the sauce. Heat oil in a pan and pan-fry the pork shreds until crispy. In a bowl, mix cream cheese with the instant coffee.

3. To assemble the dish: (a) brush pork sauce in the puff pastry, (b) fill pastry with cream cheese mixture, (c) top with *adobo* pork flakes.

COFFEE CRUSTED RIB EYE

Coffee notes form a warm and pungent arrangement with the cumin, rosemary and thyme. The cumin-and-meat combination reminds one of grilled meat dishes such as Spain's *pinchos morunos*; the rosemary and thyme are Mediterranean sunshine, and add peppery flavors with a mouth-cleansing, balsamic finish. With the butter on top, this dish is set to become a comfort food favorite, with a touch of sophistication.

Serves 1

For the butter peppercorn
butter
mixed peppercorn

For the coffee rub
2 tablespoons instant coffee powder
pinch of brown sugar
pinch of ground cumin
salt and pepper, to taste
pinch of thyme
pinch of rosemary

1 tablespoon vegetable oil
200 grams of rib eye

1. Prepare the butter peppercorn, whip the butter until light in color. Crack the peppercorns until they are coarsely ground. Fold the coarsely ground peppercorns into the whipped butter and put in a pastry bag with a star tip. Pipe out the butter peppercorn on parchment paper and chill.

2. Mix all the coffee rub ingredients in a bowl.

3. Coat the rib eye with the coffee rub.

4. In a hot pan, add vegetable oil and sear the rib eye quickly on both sides and place in the oven at 350 degrees Farenheit for 8 minutes or to your desired doneness.

5. To serve, top rib eye with chilled butter peppercorn.

BLACKENED FISH

Cajun seasoning is like a multiple-layered depth charge. Fennel seed, cumin, mustard powder and cayenne are accompanied by sage, oregano, and thyme; garlic and onion are there too. This recipe expands on it by boosting the pungent warmth of the cumin, and adds the floral, orange-peel sweetness of coriander. The thyme is there to keep things clean at the end of the mouthful. With the coffee, this makes for a muscular, yet elegant dish.

Serves 2

For the coffee spice mix
2 teaspoons Cajun spices
2 teaspoons paprika
2 teaspoons brown sugar
2 teaspoons ground cumin
2 teaspoons ground coriander
1 teaspoon dried thyme
2 teaspoons black peppercorns
2 teaspoons roasted ground coffee

1 tablespoon vegetable oil
360 grams of grouper

1. Mix all the coffee spice mixture ingredients together. Season grouper with salt and rub the spice mixture all over.

2. In a hot pan, add the vegetable oil and sear the fish on both sides. Finish cooking in the oven for 7 to 10 minutes at 275 degrees Fahrenheit.

COFFEE RAVIOLI

This is a dish that will delight the eye and the palate in equal measure. The two-tone pasta pouches are a mouth-pleasing vehicle for the burst of liquid coffee and chocolate that wait within. Another one to please choffeeholics.

Makes 15 raviolis

For the white pasta dough
1/3 cup all purpose flour, sifted
1 egg
1/2 teaspoon white sugar
pinch of salt
1 tablespoon milk

For the coffee pasta dough
1/3 cup all purpose flour, sifted
1 egg
1/2 teaspoon white sugar
pinch of salt
1 tablespoon milk
1 tablespoon instant coffee powder

For the filling
1 1/2 cups dark chocolate
1/3 cup heavy cream
2 tablespoons amaretto
1 tablespoon instant coffee
   powder
1/3 cup white sugar

For the vanilla sauce
2 egg yolks
50 grams of white sugar
1/4 cup cream
1/4 cup milk

1. In a bowl, mix all the white pasta dough ingredients together, knead and form into a ball, put dough back in the bowl and cover. Rest the dough for 30 minutes in a chiller. Do the same process to make the coffee pasta dough.

2. Roll out the white pasta dough and coffee pasta dough in a pasta machine (use the number 5 setting of the dialer). Cut each pasta sheet into .5 cm strips. Using some water, connect the pasta strips together, alternating between the white pasta and the coffee pasta. Overlap a little of each section so that they stick together properly. Sprinkle the alternating pasta sheet with flour, and then carefully pass it through the pasta machine one more time. Cut the alternating pasta sheet into 2-inch squares or floral patterns with a cookie cutter. Set aside.

3. Prepare the filling: Melt the chocolate in a bowl (do not melt chocolate over direct heat, set the bowl over a pot of simmering water). Stir in the cream, amaretto, coffee, and sugar. Chill the mixture in the refrigerator for 4 hours, until firm. Divide this mixture into 24 sections and quickly roll into small balls. Chill for another 1 hour or overnight.

4. Prepare the vanilla sauce: Mix egg yolk and sugar in a bowl. Heat the cream and milk, then gradually pour the hot liquid into the egg yolk and sugar mix. Stir constantly. Pour the mixture back into the pan and put over medium heat. Cook the mixture until thick.

5. To assemble: Take a piece of the pre-cut pasta and put a ball of the filling in the center, then top with another piece of pre-cut pasta. Press edges together to close. Blanch raviolis in boiling water for 2 minutes. Drizzle vanilla sauce over pasta before serving.

COFFEE SANS RIVAL

The nutty meringue texture gives way to the sweet, coffee-creamy unctuousness. This is a classic dessert with an elegant Philippine touch in the use of peanuts. Coffee provides a pleasing restraint on the characteristic sweetness of the dish.

Serves 10

4 eggs
1/2 cup white sugar
1 teaspoon vanilla extract
1 tablespoon cake flour
1/3 cup ground peanuts

For the coffee butter cream
1 cup butter, room temperature
1 egg
2 cups powdered sugar
3 tablespoons instant coffee powder
1 teaspoon vanilla extract

For the toppings
instant coffee powder
grated chocolate
cocoa powder

1. Separate egg whites from yolk (set yolk aside for another the dish you may make). Whip egg whites until foamy, add half of the sugar and whip to stiff peaks. Combine the remaining sugar, vanilla extract, flour, and peanuts then carefully fold this into the whipped egg whites. Spread evenly on a sheet lined with parchment paper, bake for 30 minutes at 350 degrees Fahrenheit.

2. To prepare the butter coffee cream: Cream the butter until light in color, add egg, then gradually add sugar, coffee, and vanilla extract. Mix well and set aside.

3. Cut the baked pastry into rectangles and spread the coffee butter cream on top, top with another layer of baked pastry, then spread again with the coffee butter cream. Top with a sprinkling of coffee, cocoa powder or grated chocolate.

ORANGE COFFEE JELLY

This is a recipe that reaches into the jelly delights of childhood. A bed of milky orange jelly provides pleasing accompaniment to the chilled coffee jelly dice on top. An elegant way for grown-ups to chill out with a food treat on hot days.

Serves 10

For the coffee jelly
1/3 cup unflavored gelatin
1 tablespoon instant coffee powder
2 tablespoons white sugar

For the milk orange jelly
1/3 cup unflavored gelatin
1 1/2 cups milk
zest of 1 orange
1 cinnamon stick
3 tablespoons white sugar

1. For the coffee jelly: Dissolve gelatin in 1 1/2 cups of water, bring to a simmer. Add sugar and stir constantly. Strain mixture and pour into a container. Once set, cut into small squares.

2. For the milk orange jelly: Dissolve gelatin in milk, bring to a simmer. Add orange zest, cinnamon stick, and sugar. Stir constantly. Strain mixture and pour into a container. Add the diced coffee jelly when mixture slightly thickens to prevent coffee jelly from falling to the bottom.

3. To serve: Cut jelly mix into squares and top with some coffee cream (all purpose cream whipped with a few teaspoons of instant coffee powder).

COFFEE PANNACOTTA

This recipe is another dish for lovers of creamy desserts. Firm, sweet creaminess combines with coffee flavors in this pleasing chilled dessert.

Serves 20

4 cups cream
2 cups milk
1 cup sugar
2 tablespoons vanilla beans or sticks
2 tablespoons instant coffee powder
7 pieces gelatin sheets

1. Heat cream, milk, and sugar together. Simmer for 15 minutes. Add vanilla beans and coffee.

2. In a separate bowl, put in the gelatin sheets and add enough water to cover the gelatin. Add this to the cream mixture, stir constantly and strain. Transfer mixture into round molds and chill.

3. After a few hours of chilling, you may add another layer of the pannacotta mixture, this time without the coffee powder. This will create a nice brown and white layer to your pannacotta.

4. To unmold the pannacotta, dip the molds in hot water for 10 seconds then invert onto a plate. Sprinkle with coffee powder before serving.

COFFEE INDULGENCE

This is a coffee dessert for chocolate lovers, or a chocolate dessert for lovers of coffee; the perfect dessert for coffeeholics.

Serves 4

1/3 cup cream
2 tablespoons butter
2 tablespoons white sugar
2 tablespoons glucose
1/8 cup almond slivers
3/4 cup dark chocolate
1/2 cup cream
1/2 cup butter
1/3 cup white sugar
instant coffee powder
1 1/2 teaspoons unflavored gelatin
2 tablespoons milk

For the ganache
1/2 cup cream
1/2 cup dark chocolate
3 tablespoons white sugar
2 tablespoons butter

1. Combine the cream, butter, sugar, and glucose. Mix well. Heat the cream mixture until thick. Slightly toast almonds in a pan. Pour the thickened cream mixture into the almonds. Pour this almond mixture into small prepared ring molds lined with parchment paper.

2. Melt the chocolate in a bowl (do not melt chocolate over direct heat, set the bowl over a pot of simmering water). Stir in the cream, butter, sugar and instant coffee. In a separate bowl, mix the gelatin and milk, place over a pan of hot water to dissolve. Stir the gelatin mixture into the chocolate-coffee mixture and blend well. Pour this into the ring molds half-way and let it rest for 15 minutes in the chiller. Sprinkle with some coffee powder and top with the remaining chocolate-coffee mixture. Let this rest in the chiller for 1 hour.

3. To prepare the ganache: Heat the cream, stir in the chocolate, sugar, and butter.

4. To assemble: Using a hot knife unmold the chocolate from the mold and pour the ganache over it. Let it rest in the chiller for at least 2 minutes before serving.

COFFEE BANANA TART

This is an old childhood favorite that has been adapted for adult tastes: carefree sugar and banana flavors framed by a serious, responsible taste of coffee. Benjie and Amy Lou Lizada in Davao would approve of this recipe, continuing their family tradition of bananas and coffee.

Makes 15 tarts

For the pastry dough
1 1/2 cups all purpose flour, sifted
1 teaspoon white sugar
2/3 cup butter, cold
1 egg yolk
3 tablespoons milk, cold

For the filling
1/4 cup white sugar
2 teaspoons instant coffee powder
1 tablespoon butter
5 pieces ripe bananas

1. In a bowl, mix flour and sugar. Cut butter into small pieces and add into the flour mixture. Rub together until mixture becomes sandlike in texture. Add the egg yolk then add the milk slowly. Mix to form a dough. Place the dough on a paper lined sheet pan and roll out as flat as possible. Cover and refrigerate dough for 20 to 30 minutes.

2. Brush several mini tart pans with butter. Remove chilled dough from refrigerator and gently press dough against the sides and bottom of mini tart pans. Do not stretch the dough too much, it should be 1/8 inch thick. Put wax paper on top of each tart pan and top with some coffee beans for weight. Bake in oven for 5 minutes at 300 degrees Fahrenheit.

3. Prepare the filling: caramelize sugar with 1/4 cup of water. Add instant coffee, butter, and stir in sliced bananas.

4. To assemble: Arrange the caramelized bananas on the baked tart crust. Pour some caramelized sauce on top. Bake in oven for 5 minutes at 300 degrees Fahrenheit. To serve, top with cream and a coffee bean.

GINGER, COFFEE & GREEN TEA FLAN

This dish is an innovative reinterpretation of crème brulée. The rich, sweet flavors of the original are layered with the cleansing notes of ginger, and made invigorating with the caffeine and flavors of green tea and coffee. The result is a subtle, firmly defined alloy of flavors.

Serves 4

1 cup milk
1 teaspoon ginger, peeled and crushed
2 teaspoons instant coffee powder
1 bag green tea
2 tablespoons cream
1 teaspoon vanilla extract
1/3 cup sugar
3 egg yolks

For caramelized coffee beans
2 tablespoons white sugar
6 coffee beans
1 tablespoon butter

brown sugar

1. Bring the milk, ginger, and coffee to a boil. Remove milk mixture from heat and add green tea bag. Let it seep for 2 minutes. Remove tea bag and ginger, stir in cream and vanilla extract.

2. Cream the sugar and egg yolk in separate bowl, then gradually stir in milk mixture. Strain with a fine strainer. Pour mixture into a ramekin, and then place the ramekin in a food pan with hot water. Bake for 1 hour at 275 degrees Fahrenheit. Refrigerate after.

3. For the caramelized coffee beans: melt the sugar in 2 tablespoons of water, add coffee beans and caramelize. Stir in butter until well blended.

4. To assemble: sprinkle brown sugar on top of the flan (you may use a blow torch to caramelize the sugar). Garnish with the caramelized coffee beans.

COFFEE CHARLOTTE

Flavors combine in an elaborate arrangement where citrus zests provide a hint of freshness to the warmth of coffee, cinnamon, almonds and chili, with it all riding on a pleasant texture of cream. A delight for those who enjoy creamy desserts.

Serves 6

For the cream mixture
1 1/2 cups heavy cream
1 tablespoon amaretto
1 tablespoon vanilla extract
1/2 cup white sugar
1 teaspoon orange zest
1 teaspoon lemon zest
1 tablespoon unflavored gelatin

For the coffee mixture
3 tablespoons instant coffee powder
pinch of chili powder
pinch of ground cinnamon
2 tablespoons amaretto

30 pieces ladyfinger cookies

For the topping
cocoa powder
instant coffee powder

1. Prepare the cream mixture: Whip the cream until it forms stiff peaks. In a separate bowl, combine the amaretto, vanilla extract and sugar. Fold amaretto mix, orange and lemon zest in the whipped cream. Add a few tablespoons of water in the gelatin and put on low heat for a few minutes. Fold this into the cream mixture. Set aside.

2. Melt the instant coffee in 1 cup of hot water; add chili powder, ground cinnamon, and amaretto.

3. To assemble: Dip the ladyfinger in the coffee mixture. Then arrange this in a ramekin, alternating with the cream mixture. Top with a sprinkling of cocoa powder and instant coffee powder.

COFFEE TRUFFLE

The classic chocolate truffle is rich in chocolate and butter flavors. This recipe produces a truffle where chocolate and coffee are held together with amaretto almonds, making for an intensely pleasing three-note chord of flavor. Coffeeholics take note.

Makes 8 to 10 truffles

For the center
1 1/2 cups dark chocolate
1/3 cup heavy cream
2 tablespoons amaretto
1 tablespoon instant coffee powder
1/3 cup white sugar

For the coating
1 1/2 cups dark chocolate
1 1/2 cups white chocolate

chopped pistachios
chopped hazel nuts
chopped almonds

1. To prepare the center: Melt the chocolate in a bowl (do not melt chocolate over direct heat, set the bowl over a pot of simmering water). Stir in the cream, amaretto, coffee, and sugar. Chill the mixture in the refrigerator for 4 hours, until firm. Divide this mixture into 24 sections and quickly roll into a ball. Chill for another 1 hour or overnight.

2. Melt the chocolate for coating in separate bowls. Using two forks, carefully dip the center truffles one at a time into the melted chocolate – either the dark or white chocolate or both. Place the truffles on wax paper to set. You may also roll the center truffles in chopped pistachios, hazels nuts or almonds.

Coffee soaps, scrubs and salts have been the rage in recent years due to coffee's ability to exfoliate, soothe, deodorize, and heal.

HOME MADE COFFEE PRODUCTS

Studies performed at the University of New Jersey have found that caffeine can reduce the risk of skin cancer caused by ultraviolet (UV) radiation when applied topically to skin. Earlier studies have postulated that caffeine slowed down DNA repair following damage resulting UV irradiation and, by slowing it down, was allowing the repair to be more precise, avoiding the mutations that can lead to cancer. This particular benefit has been ascribed to the antioxidants present in coffee.

In addition to these clinical surveys, coffee has been used for centuries to detoxify and de-stress.

The Japanese soak in large vats of coffee grounds, expressly for this reason. Coffee scrubs and salts have been the rage in recent years due to coffee's ability to exfoliate, soothe, deodorize, and heal. There are even coffee devotees who claim that rubbing coffee grounds on the scalp will cure dandruff and can actually regrow hair (although no clinical data has been reported to prove this).

Natural caffeine can reduce the incidence of acne and heal recovery from it. Continued use can fade age spots and reduce wrinkles on the skin, and has also been known to provide relief from skin allergies.

Main ingredients needed for making coffee lotion: lotion base and instant coffee powder.

COFFEE LOTION

2 cups unscented body lotion base
4 drops of coffee fragrance oil
2 drop of vanilla fragrance oil
2 teaspoons of instant coffee powder

Gently mix body lotion base with 2:1 ratio of coffee and vanilla fragrance oils, then mix with instant coffee powder. Start with a lesser amount of fragrance and build up to suit your scent needs.

COFFEE BODY SCRUB

This beauty treatment helps revitalize, detoxify and refresh your whole body so that you can achieve that blissful glow without ever having to take a sip. Coffee is an excellent skin cleanser that also improves circulation and skin tone.

Coffee is granular and feels nice on the skin but the caffeine has added benefits. Applied topically, coffee helps to redistribute fat cells and decrease the formation of cellulite. It also acts as a vasorestrictor, tightening and shrinking blood vessels thereby helping eliminate varicose veins. It has been used for years in spas in Hawaii and on the coast of Bali.

1/3 cup coarsely ground coffee
1 tablespoon instant coffee powder
1/3 cup raw sugar or sea salt
2/3 cups massage oil

Mix all ingredients together. Take a hot shower to moisten your skin and open your pores. Using wide, circular motions, rub the coffee exfoliant onto your skin with strong, even pressure. Shower off, pat skin dry, and apply a thin layer of your favorite body lotion.

You can use many kinds of oil, including jojoba oil, safflower oil, apricot kernel oil, grape seed oil, even olive or vegetable oil. The use of mineral oil (baby oil) is not recommended as it will not penetrate the skin like the other oils.

Main ingredients needed for making coffee body scrub: salt, oil, instant coffee powder, sugar.

COFFEE SOAP

Anyone who loves the scent of coffee will love this soap. But it's also great for cooks because the coffee absorbs odors like garlic and fish.

1 cup soybean oil
1/2 cup coconut oil
1/2 cup olive oil
1/2 cup double strength liquid coffee, instead of water
1/4 cup lye
1-2 tablespoons ground coffee or instant coffee

1. Use safety gloves and goggles or eyeglasses.

2. Weigh the required amount of coffee (made with distilled water is best) into one of the pitchers. To do this, place an empty pitcher on the scale and set to zero. Now measure the amount of coffee.

3. Using the same method as above, weigh the lye needed in the second pitcher.

4. Carefully pour the lye into the pitcher containing the coffee. You must avoid splashing-this is the most dangerous step! And pour in very slowly. Never add the water to the lye.

5. Stir solution gently with a wooden spoon until dissolved. Make sure you have sufficient ventilation. Resist the temptation to lean

Basic ingredients needed for making coffee soap: ground coffee or instant coffee and double strength liquid coffee.

over the pitcher to get a good look. You do not want to breathe anywhere near this container. The smell will be very strong.

6. While the lye is cooling, melt the fats. The temperature of both must eventually be brought to 100 degrees simultaneously. If the lye solution cools too much, put the pitcher in a pan or bowl of hot water.

7. Double-check the temperatures of the lye and fat solutions to be sure they are 100-110 degrees (equal temperature is desired).

8. While stirring the fats, pour the lye solution into the melted fat/oil in a thin stream. Stir continuously to ensure the lye mixes into the fat.

9. Continue stirring in a carefully manner to avoid splashing. The mixture should start thickening. You will eventually see "trailings" or lines on the surface. This could take 20 minutes to an hour, usually closer to one hour. Be careful when using hand mixers as they can speed things up too much.

10. Add the used coffee grounds for every pound of soap in your recipe. You can add a coffee fragrance if you like, though the coffee scent will come through lightly even without it.

11. Pour this liquid soap into your large plastic container mold. Put the lid on and wrap with the towel.

12. Put the wrapped mold in a warm place and allow to set for 48 hours.

13. After 48 hours, unwrap the mold. The soap should still be warm. If the surface is still very soft, leave lid off for a day. When firm it is ready to be removed from the mold.

14. Remove soap from mold. To do this, first pull the plastic mold away from the soap on all sides. Then, turn the mold over onto the needlepoint screen or plastic. If it doesn't fall out of the mold, push down on the upside down mold and it should pop out. You should have a nice clean block of soap ready to be cut into bars.

15. First, score the surface where the cuts will be made. Then, warm the knife to be used in water. Dry the knife and cut the block into bars of soap.

16. The hand-cut bars still need to cure. They will become lighter in weight and slightly smaller. Place them on the plastic needlepoint screen for about three weeks.

COFFEE DYE

Coffee even has its uses in the fashion industry. Internationally recognized and most sought-after Philippine designer Rajo Laurel started using coffee as a dye while at design school. Coffee provides depth of color, as well a pleasing brown, caramel finish. It works on fabrics and paper, and is often used to create an antique or vintage feel.

Rajo´s own coffee dye formula is very simple. Every pound of fabric requires 4 cups of water, one cup of instant coffee powder and half a cup of salt. The salt stabilizes the dyeing pigment, and facilitates its adhesion to the material. The longer the fabric is allowed to soak in the dye mix, the darker the resulting color. If using instant coffee, bear in mind the differences in shade between different types, such as Decaf or Premium blends, as these will result in different intensities of shade.

INDEX

ENABLING FILIPINOS THROUGH THE YEARS

From the careful selection of the coffee beans to the special state-of-the-art roasting process, NESCAFÉ makes sure our consumers experience only quality – from bean to cup.

The NESCAFÉ Filipinos enjoy every day is a product of a rigorous manufacturing process that includes sorting, roasting, and tasting to ensure that it meets the strict NESCAFÉ quality standards established all over the world. The result is NESCAFÉ made from 100% pure coffee, which means it contains no additives and no artificial flavors.

And we never stop improving our coffee. Our global Research & Development Network is always at work to further improve the NESCAFÉ taste and aroma, and to create new ways for our consumers to enjoy it.

This is perhaps why NESCAFÉ has become so much a part of the lives of generations of Filipinos. Through the years, in good times and in bad, NESCAFÉ has kept you company -- whether you are alone, relaxing and reflecting in between sips of coffee, or while enjoying animated conversations with family and friends as you savor cup after cup of NESCAFÉ. And while enjoying your cup of coffee, isn't it great to note that NESCAFÉ, which has been part of your daily routine, makes you more alert and focused while providing you the antioxidant protection you need?

But our passion and dedication for coffee do not start with the bean and end with the cup. Everything starts with the hardworking Filipino coffee farmers, whose efforts make possible every cup of NESCAFÉ. Today, NESCAFÉ sources coffee from around 30,000 Filipino farmers, and indirectly benefits some 300,000 more who are in some way involved in the planting, harvesting, or processing and trading of coffee. As the leading coffee brand in the Philippines, NESCAFÉ is committed to support Filipino coffee farmers through various programs to encourage them to grow coffee in a sustainable way – from regularly providing them training on efficient farming techniques, to giving them access to high quality coffee seedlings, and buying coffee beans directly from them at a suitable price based on prevailing world market prices. Through these, we hope to help grow the local coffee industry, and raise awareness for Philippine coffee.

There are certainly many ways to enjoy a good cup of coffee, and many moments to savor the coffee experience. NESCAFÉ hopes to be part of many more moments in the lives of the Filipino people in the years to come.

ACKNOWLEDGMENTS

We journeyed far and wide in our research, and travelers have a debt of gratitude to those who helped along the way. Many gave time, provided access to their homes and places of work, gave patient explanation and generously shared personal recollections.

In Manila, we thank Corin, head waitress at Panciteria Lido; Bill Luz, Treasurer of the Philippine Coffee Board and recent new member of the coffee-growing community; Robert Francisco at Boyd's Coffee for his enthusiastic walk-through of coffee roasting and espresso making; Ken Tan and Owen Tiam for providing early research and photography; and Aleli Magtibay for providing her expertise as a nutritionist.

In Malaybalay, Bukidnon, we met with pest-control expert Francisco Laigo who shared childhood experiences in the Luzon Cordillera. Pio and Lionila Secadron made time to meet with us there too. Mario Ledesma took us to Ragus farm, and impressed us with his botanical expertise.

In Davao, Andrew Lui provided the local feel for the city's cafes and markets. Gatchi Gatchalian and Amy Lou Lizada introduced us to Durian Gatchpuccino and Bananapuccino respectively.

In Sagada, ex-mayor Tom Killip, Pancho Masferre and Villia Jefremovas provided unpublished detail and anecdote. We thank Julius Sabala, Ricky Sta. Cruz, and Clester Macabeo for keeping us safe on roads that were not always user-friendly.

In addition, we thank the following individuals and organizations:

Father Savio Sicuan and Dom Myron of Monk's Blend
Rajo Laurel of the House of Laurel
Santi Macutay of The Manila Hotel
Nikki Verzo of Coffee Bean & Tea Leaf
Raymund Isaac

Bruno Olierhoek, Jules H. del Pilar, Noy Dy-Liacco, Joel Lumagbas, Prox Cortejos, Jay Gatchalian, Zenon Alenton, Cate Reyes, Benhur Ignacio, Ernesto Mercado, Rudy Trillanes, Titus Fernandez, TinTin Siapno, Jane Pronstroller, Paul and Tedd Belamide, Tonette Escario, Jon Antonio, Aldous Castro, Dr. Siday Peñaranda, Dr. Raymond de Villa, Gian Trinidad, Pamela Antig, Mr. & Mrs. Ernesto Mendoza, Gil Pansoy, Harold Depositor, Albert Geduque, and Ariel Famucal.

Panciteria Lido, Cabalen, Café By the Ruins, Maria's Buko Pies, Walter Mart, and Philippine Mountain Coffee.